International Relations In Global Era :

Concept and Revision of Public Diplomacy Around the World

JALAL NALI

ABSTRACT

This research study intend to examine the public's perception of foreign countries influenced by news coverage. This study explores the international PR activities of foreign governments that targets specific civil societies in order to influence their local media portrayal, and, consequently, citizens' perception of these foreign countries. Public diplomacy is not merely about advocating and promoting political and economic goals to the international publics; it is, instead, about relationship building between nations and cultures through better communication. Therefore, public diplomacy is the public face of traditional diplomacy. This study is one of a few that quantified public relations and tries to find empirical evidence of PR influence on the news media and public perception. International PR efforts operationally defined and quantified from the publicly available government-generated data.

DEDICATION

"It is very unnerving to be proven wrong, particularly when you are really right and the person who is really wrong is the one who is proving you wrong and proving himself, wrongly, right. Right?"

Lemony Snicket

Special dedication to my missed dad and his unconditional support; and to many inspiring friends working in diplomatic missions around the world.

TABLE OF CONTENTS

CHAPTER 1: INTRODUCTION

Background of the Study

Public diplomacy is a concept that links with booming development of diplomatic activity in new and different levels of government activities. The taxonomy of international relations has had to reinvent itself with the emergence of new actors with power to influence the performance and direction of international acts. The Westphalian system, based on the unity of language and territory under a single command, diluted to the detriment of new entrants who are likely to influence international relations. The foreign policy and international image no longer the monopoly of States has ceded part of its space to non-core administrative legal actors. Wang (2006) notes that "public diplomacy is not merely about advocating and promoting political and economic goals to the international publics; it is, instead, about relationship building between nations and cultures through better communication" (p. 93). To Wang, therefore, public diplomacy is the "public face of traditional diplomacy" (p. 91).

Previous studies have uncovered two types of public diplomacy efforts: (1) information dissemination through the mass media and other means; and (2) cultural diplomacy. First, governments can reach foreign publics by disseminating information through the mass media (e.g., through public relations campaigns in mass media) or by directly delivering information (e.g., print or video materials) to the general public without mass media intervention[1]. The U.S., for instance, reaches out to the Middle East through American Corner, an organized collection of Internet-accessible computers and books on American subjects installed in several Middle Eastern universities. It is considered to be a cost-effective and safe way to help students and the general public know more about American culture, society, and politics.

Government-sponsored radio and television broadcasts in foreign markets are another way to reach foreign publics. For instance, during the Cold War, the Voice of America, Radio Free Europe, and Radio Liberty were launched to convey a positive American image to specific target countries. Today, in response to negative publicity in the Muslim media - the so-called Al Jazeera effect - the Bush administration subsidizes a variety of media channels, including radio stations, satellite channels, websites, and teen magazines to directly reach the Muslim world. Second, governments can reach foreign publics through a variety of cultural channels used in public diplomacy efforts. Cultural diplomacy, or public diplomacy through cultural channels,

[1] Nam, Seungji. "Independent Diplomacy between North Korea and China Folllowing the 20th Communist Congress of the Soviet Union." Order No. 1479925, University of Southern California, 2010. In PROQUESTMS ProQuest Dissertations & Theses Full Text, http://search.proquest.com/docview/748231594?accountid=120 85.

focuses on long-term relationship-building instead of conflict resolution or immediate information delivery[2]. Schneider (2006) notes that "culture provides a means to expand upon ideas and images created by the market" (p. 158). Gilboa (2000) counts "cultural and scientific exchanges of students, scholars, intellectuals, and artists; participation in festivals and exhibitions; building and maintaining cultural centres; teaching a language; and establishing local friendship leagues and trade associations" as cultural diplomatic activities (p. 291).

Schneider (2006) argues that even during the Cold War, artists in the Soviet Union, such as dancers with the Bolshoi and Kirov ballets impressed the American public in spite of ideological differences between the two countries. Artistic and cultural exchanges between the U.S. and the Soviet Union were regarded as "a means of counteracting isolationism and increasing understanding between the two countries" (p. 157). As part of its ongoing efforts, to promote a positive image in Middle Eastern countries, the State Department's Middle East Partnership Initiative promotes the ideology of democracy and women's rights. In Jordan, for example, the U.S. sponsors a student exchange or education program targeted at teenagers that involves after-school English classes and U.S. embassy tours.

[2] Scott, Kendra U. "Embassies as Art Institutions Symbols of Exchange." Order No. 1509762, American University, 2012. In PROQUESTMS ProQuest Dissertations & Theses Full Text, http://search.proquest.com/docview/1015014627?accountid=12085.

Robison (2005) explains that these cultural programs are designed to allow students in Muslim countries to experience "real images of Americans rather than the ones they see in Al Jazeera" (p. 5).

The European Union, since its inception, has been criticized for its lack of unity. The effectiveness of its public diplomacy has come into question, evidenced by a lack of understanding, and more importantly, interest in, the EU, which has recently manifested in a weakening of relations with the U.S. This paper will look at the issue in terms of the EU's voice, how it is seen and interpreted by non-EU publics, reasons for this and how perception may be changed. Various reports say the EU's lack of a unified voice and message is the biggest challenge to its public diplomacy, and if it does not do more to rectify this problem of unity, it will never be the major global power it hopes to be; more specifically, it will continue to lose the beneficial and robust relationship it has fostered with the U.S[3].

The public diplomacy actions and capabilities of the EU in the world, and specifically the U.S., through interviews and literature about EU public diplomacy; narrowing down specific problems and recommendations; looking at how the EU is, or is not, addressing the question of speaking with one

---

[3] Sevin, Hasan Efe. "Making New Friends? Relational Public Diplomacy as a Foreign Policy Instrument." Order No. 3631071, American University, 2014. In PROQUESTMS ProQuest Dissertations & Theses Full Text, http://search.proquest.com/docview/1564442089?accountid=12085.

voice; and understanding under what assumptions such recommendations are made and deemed valid. It is not the lack of unity that is missing from EU public diplomacy, but rather, the way it frames its own image, as a nation-state, which it is not, causing non-EU publics to have incorrect perceptions and expectations, which can never be fulfilled. It will offer recommendations for a new frame more suited to the EU's identity: a supranational institution, and ways to present this to the American public. The European Union set up following World War II under the desire for putting an end to the bloody wars that frequently erupted between European neighbours, has throughout its history been an experiment in governance and integration. In 1951, under the Treaty of Paris, its six founders, Belgium, France, Germany, Italy, Luxembourg and the Netherlands, united into the European Coal and Steel Community for economic and security benefits[4].

In 1957 they integrated deeper, economically, into the European Economic Community. In 1973, the first new members, Denmark, Ireland and the United Kingdom, joined, followed by most of Western and Central Europe into the 1990s and 2000s. The last crop of members, some of who were Soviet Union republics, joined in 2004 and 2007.

[4] Wang, Szuhai J. "Public Diplomacy and Organizational Conflict: A Study of Taiwanese Government Information Offices in the United States." Order No. 3430719, University of La Verne, 2010. In PROQUESTMS ProQuest Dissertations & Theses Full Text, http://search.proquest.com/docview/795221111?accountid=120 85.

The union, now with 27 member countries, has proved prosperous for its members as they have benefited from each other's resources and from new opportunities presented to them through their collective strengths. The EU adopted and refined a set of criteria for those wishing to join to ensure that all members maintained certain standards in the areas of governance, economy and democratic norms. Though it was primarily an economic partnership at its beginning, the EU now unites its members in various policies and structures and has its own set of institutions and leaders.

The integration process has not always been a smooth one and the EU continues to wrestle with problems of cohesion. As the EU borders have moved further East disagreements have arisen. Some have questioned the benefit of admitting member countries who have nothing to offer the group, whose human rights records are nothing short of atrocious, and whose economies, never able to stand on their own after the Soviet breakup, have been even further ravaged by the recent economic crisis. The EU now is a true hodgepodge of characters – different languages cultures, beliefs, religions, people and experiences – united across the European continent to foster "peace, prosperity and freedom for its 498 million citizens — in a fairer, safer world. Throughout its development the EU has presented itself as a unique economic, social and political enterprise. It has sought to be a leader in modern policy-making, promoting itself as an example for developing and future regional unions[5].

In this respect, the practice of public diplomacy has always been an important aspect of its international diplomacy strategy. Bruce Gregory's definition of public diplomacy here: Public diplomacy is a coherent blend of activities used by governments, groups, and individuals to understand attitudes, cultures, and mediated environments; engage in a dialogue of ideas between people and institutions, advise political leaders on public opinion implications of policy choices, influence attitudes and behaviour through communication strategies, actions, and messages, and measure results.

The EU's individual member countries have had varied experiences with public diplomacy; what started out as a necessary means to counteract foreign publics' negative perceptions of them, has blossomed into an integral part of their foreign policies. Germany used its public diplomacy to normalize relations and improve its reputation, tainted by the atrocities of World War II; France, in much the same way, used public diplomacy to save face after its humiliation in the war. More recently, new EU members, or those desiring to be part of the union, like Poland and Turkey, have used public

---

[5] Vibber, Kelly S. "Advocates Or Adversaries? an Exploration of Communicative Actions of within-Border Foreign Publics and their Affect on the Host Country's Soft Power." Order No. 3636675, Purdue University, 2014. In PROQUESTMS ProQuest Dissertations & Theses Full Text, http://search.proquest.com/docview/1615376857?accountid=12085.

diplomacy for specific foreign policy goals, to elevate their image and take their case for accession to the public. Smaller countries, like Malta, have used public diplomacy mechanisms to raise the world's awareness about their existence, with the hopes of stimulating tourism[6].

The EU is seen as uniquely equipped to conduct public diplomacy because it possesses vast amounts of soft power, defined here as the ability to obtain desired effects through cooption and attraction, the "power of seduction," and hard power, the ability to influence behaviours through the use of economic incentives and or military strength; though it must be noted that the lack of an EU military force has caused some to doubt the EU's capabilities in the areas of defence and security. The ability to combine the two powers into successful international strategies is smart power.

The EU's smart power is achieved through the combination of the individual states' separate abilities, both in and outside of government, in soft and hard power areas. The European continent, home to some of the world's most famous artists, musicians, rulers and sights, among other hallmarks of the arts and history, has a wealth of cultural

[6] Ubelaker, Lisa A. "The Impossible Americas: Argentina, Ecuador, and the Geography of U.S. Mass Media, 1938--1948." Order No. 3572007, Yale University, 2013. In PROQUESTMS ProQuest Dissertations & Theses Full Text, http://search.proquest.com/docview/1433929786?accountid=12 085.

resources for self promotion at its disposal. Because the EU is endowed in this soft power area, its hard power sources and capabilities are often overlooked or taken for granted. The plethora of non-governmental organizations and actors in the EU who conduct public diplomacy through their international relationships and business agreements adds to the EU's smart power. Regular citizens also have the capacity to act as mechanisms of public diplomacy through their interactions with the many tourists who visit their cities.

Statement of the Problem

Today, it is widely believed that a positive national image enables a nation to achieve a more advantageous position in global economic and political competition. A positive national image may drive other nations' foreign policies in favour of a country, increase revenues from products, and draw tourists and foreign investment. Moreover, as the attacks of September 11, 2001 and have shown, severe antagonistic feelings from foreign publics may even threaten national security[7].

---

[7] Stapleton, Bradford Ian. "The Strategic Consequences of Military Quagmires: An Examination of War-Weariness Theory." Order No. 3637502, University of California, Los Angeles, 2014. In PROQUESTMS ProQuest Dissertations & Theses Full Text, http://search.proquest.com/docview/1617458330?accountid=12085.

Because a positive national image is regarded as national capital, many governments are starting to improve their national image by directly communicating with foreign publics. Wang (2006) argues that national reputation is an indication of a nation's power and strength. Other scholars Jervis, (1970; Nye, (2004) have emphasized the pivotal role of a positive national image as a form of "soft power," as opposed to the "hard" military or economic forms of power. Nye (2004) defines soft power as "the ability to get what you want through attraction rather than coercion or payments" (p. x). It can be achieved by "the attractiveness of a country's culture, political ideals, and policies" (p. x). Hard power, on the other hand, is generally represented by economic and military sanctions. Nye (2004), however, also argues that hard and soft power must complement each other to achieve national goals.

Public diplomacy is one way by which governments can improve their soft power by going directly to foreign publics. Over the past decades, government-to-government interactions through political leaders such presidents, prime ministers, and ambassadors had typically been considered the most efficient form of diplomacy. However, many governments are now experimenting with various ways of reaching foreign publics through the media and through other ways because they recognize that the positive opinion of foreign publics can improve national image and, consequently, influence favourable foreign policies toward their countries[8].

---

[8] Schumacher, Leslie Rogne. "A "Lasting Solution": The

This study aims to investigate (1) how international PR activities conducted by a government influence the image of a country as perceived by foreign publics and portrayed in the foreign news media, and (2) how the public's perception of foreign countries is influenced by this news coverage. Following Lee's (2004) proposed path of influence as shown in Figure 1, this study explores the international PR activities of foreign governments that target the United States in order to influence U.S. media portrayal of foreign countries, and, consequently, U.S. citizens' perception of these foreign countries.

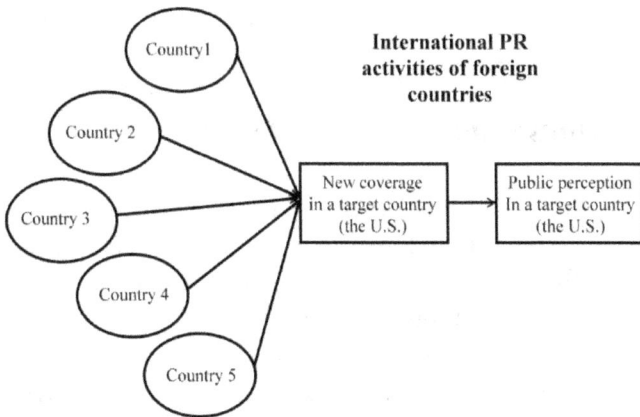

Eastern Question and British Imperialism, 1875-1878." Order No. 3523024, University of Minnesota, 2012. In PROQUESTMS ProQuest Dissertations & Theses Full Text, http://search.proquest.com/docview/1037992277?accountid=12085.

Figure 1. National images of foreign countries perceived by U.S. news media and public. *Adapted from A theoretical model of national image processing and international public relations, by S. Lee, 2004, p. 4.*

Aims and Objectives of the Study

This research study intended to examine the public's perception of foreign countries influenced by news coverage. This study explores the international PR activities of foreign governments that target the United States in order to influence U.S. media portrayal of foreign countries, and, consequently, U.S. citizens' perception of these foreign countries

Hypotheses and Research Question

From the background of the study, statement of the problem and available literature (discussed later), this study suggests a model illustrating the relationships among international public relations efforts by a foreign country, the U.S. news coverage of the foreign country, and the U.S. public's perception of a given country (Figure 2). The model will be tested using the U.S. as the target country whose public opinion many foreign countries aim to influence[9]. Following common public relations

---

[9] Rimner, Steffen. "The Asian Origins of Global Narcotics Control, c. 1860-1909." Order No. 3627071, Harvard

objectives, it is assumed that these countries employ communication strategies and techniques to gain positive portrayals in the U.S. media. Such positive portrayals translated to favourable American public opinion about the source countries.

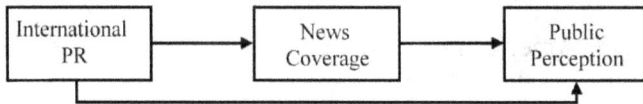

Figure 2. The flow model of international PR, news coverage, and public perceptions

Based on the problem statement, this study posits the following hypotheses in regard to the relationships among the three elements. The first set of hypotheses proposes the international public relations efforts of a foreign country will influence the U.S. news coverage in terms of the prominence and valence of U.S. media coverage of the source countries. Thus:

H1-a: More international public relations efforts will lead to more prominent news coverage of a foreign country in the U.S. media.

University, 2014. In PROQUESTMS ProQuest Dissertations & Theses Full Text, http://search.proquest.com/docview/1557746398?accountid=12 085.

H1-b: More international public relations efforts will lead to more positive news coverage of a foreign country in the U.S. media.

The second set of hypotheses assumes that the extent to which a foreign country is prominently and positively portrayed in the U.S. news media will affect American public perception of this foreign country in the U.S. Hence,

H2-a: The more prominent news coverage a foreign country receives, the more the country will be perceived by the U.S. public as significant to their country and to their lives.

H2-b: The more positively a foreign country is portrayed in the U.S. news media, the more positively the country will be perceived by the U.S. public. The more negatively a foreign country is portrayed in the U.S. news media, the more negatively the country will be perceived by the U.S. public.

The third set of hypotheses assumes that the international public relations efforts of a foreign country will influence U.S. public perception.

H3-a: International public relations efforts by a foreign country will be positively correlated to the perceived significance of that country among the U.S. public.

H3-b: International public relations efforts by a foreign country will increase the positive feelings of the U.S. public toward that country.

The six suggested hypotheses are illustrated in Figure 3. Each arrow linking the two variables represents one of six hypotheses. In addition to the six hypotheses, the following research question is posed:

RQ 1: To what extent does the proposed model (Figure 3) explain the relationships among the international public relations efforts of a foreign country, news coverage of the country (i.e., prominence and valence) in the U.S. media, and U.S. public perceptions of the country (i.e., cognitive and affective evaluations)?

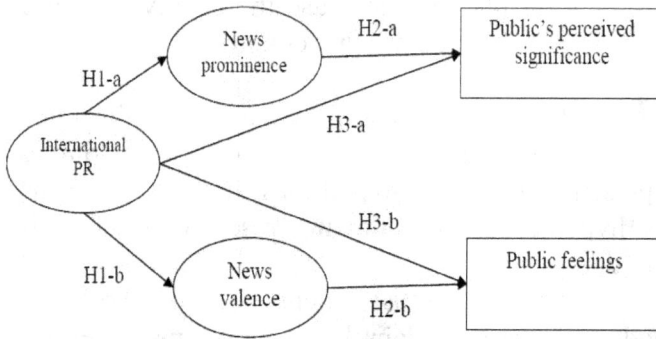

Figure 3. Flow chart of variables involved in the six hypotheses

CHAPTER 2: LITERATURE REVIEW

Public Relations

One of the most cited definitions of public relations comes from Cutlip, Centre, and Broom (2000), who suggested that public relations is a "management function that establishes and maintains mutually beneficial relationships between an organization and the public's on whom its success or failure depends" (p. 6). It can be quickly understood that the main focus here is on establishing and maintaining mutually beneficial relationships with an organization and its publics. Heath (2001) also saw public relations as a management function that "rhetorically adapts organizations to people's interest and people's interests to organizations by co-creating meaning and co-managing cultures to achieve mutually beneficial relationships" (p. 36). Smith (2005) also defined public relations as a management function, which focuses on "long-term patterns of interaction between an organization and all of its publics, both supportive and non supportive, seeking to enhance those relationships and thus generate mutual understanding, goodwill and support" (p. 347). The emphasis on relationships is emphasized in all definitions cited above.

According to Stephen Walt (1998), it is important for the policy makers to consider the study of international relations important. However, the author suggests that there is a significant difference between theory and policies. International relations can be seen as a competition between the realist, liberal, and radical traditions. Now it is the choice of the states which theory they devise the policies. For example, keeping in view the debate about the NATO expansion, one may look from the pragmatic approach that NATO expansion is an effort to extend the western influence, however, according to the Walt, the liberal perspective of this expansion is to reinforce the democracies of central Europe and extend the NATO's conflict (p. 30). Therefore, Walt emphasizes that, in international relations, no single approach can be used to understand the world politics[10].

Referring to the view of Stephen (2004), it can be said that the policy makers pay less attention to the theoretical literature in international relations and scholars are not interested in the policy related work. This behaviour is unfortunate as the theory is essential to the crafting the state enlightened policies. The focus of many policy makers is often on relying on the flawed theory leading to the policy disaster (p. 23). Therefore, theory is important to diagnose the events, and analyzing their influence on various policies[11].

---

[10] Walt, S. (1998) "International Relations: One World, Many Theories," Foreign Policy (Spring): 29–46.
[11] Walt, S. (2004), "The relationship between theory and Policy in international relations", Kennedy School of Government, Harvard University, Cambridge, Massachusetts 02138; pp. 1-28.

Similarly, Hans J. Morgenthau presents a theory if international politics where, according to him, the issues in international politics arise as the modern political theory is the contest between various theories. One of the theories is that a moral and rational administrative order comes from the abstract principles that are valid and they can be achieved now. Such school of thought trusts in reform, education, and the use of force to remedy these defects. Another theory known as political realism believes that politics is governed by the laws having their roots in human nature, to improve the society the foremost priority is to understand the laws by which the society lives. As there are various facets of the imperfect nature, political realism recognized that to understand one of them, one has to deal with its own terms[12].

Keeping in view the importance of understanding of international relations, John. Mearsheimer and Stephen M. Walt (2003) give an account of the decision taken about Iraq war and its impact on U.S. there had been a conflict between the groups who favoured Iraq war and those who despised it. The war of Iraq can be categorized as a preventive war which required some serious decisions on the part of the U.S government. According to the authors, those who favoured the war were rational aggressors. They were in favour of

---

[12] Morgenthau, H. J.(1973). "Politics Among Nations: The Struggle for Power and Peace". New York: Knopf. pp. n.a.

selling a preventive war so that they must try to make the peace seem unacceptably dangerous[13].

In the basis, of the foregoing discussion, it can be said that the universal relation theory is often important to device the policies; however, the theories cannot be replicated to the devised policies all the time as evident from many occasions in world politics, now the questions are to what extend do the policy makers should rely on the international relation theories? And if these theories give an accurate account of the political problems in devising strategies. The two are significant question that the intentional relation needs to answer so that the theory and practice can be integrated and understood better.

According to the researcher Smith in 2000, explanatory theory includes neo realism, neo liberalism and much of mainstream constructivism. It is characterized, above all, by positivist premises, explanatory theorists, committed to the view that the social world is amenable to the same kinds of analysis, as the natural world, to a separation between facts, and, values for uncovering patterns, and, regularities that occur in these concepts. Thus, explanatory theorists might be expected to apply their theories in accordance with the covering law model of explanation, in which an episode, explained by subsuming it under general laws, i.e. by showing

---

[13] Mearsheimer, J, Walt, S. (2003), "An Unnecessary War", Foreign Policy, No. 134, Carnegie Endowment for International Peace, pp. 50-59.

that it occurred in accordance with those laws, in virtue of the realization of certain specified antecedent conditions. Neo realists seek to show how balancing behaviour, driven by the anarchic structure of the international system. Neo liberals seek to show how institutions facilitate cooperation under anarchy, and, mainstream constructivists seek to show how states' interests, and, identities, socially constructed. If applied in accordance with the covering law model, these theories would be used to show that an outcome was to be expected because the specified antecedent conditions fulfilled. In such circumstances, the outcome could be deduced from the theory's reported covering laws.

Some theorists have attempted to apply explanatory theories deductively. For example, researcher known as Posen in 1984 made an attempt to compare organization theory, and, neorealist balance of power theory 'by deducing propositions' about French, British, and, German military doctrine during the interwar period. However, he is unable to make these deductions: in order to construct neorealist hypotheses about military doctrine, he has to pull the theory in the direction of "political realism" or "Real politic'" with which, closely identified, but not synonymous. Thus, he describes the two 'families of hypotheses that he tests, not as propositions deduced from theoretical assumptions, but as representing two distinct perspectives on state behaviour. In fact, he accepts that his use of the terms organization theory and balance of power theory may be somewhat misleading, though he insists that they do indicate the general origins of his hypotheses. His problem is that neo realism does not specify balancing behaviour in sufficient detail that it is possible to deduce what sorts of military doctrines are required.

The idea that explanatory theories are not, in fact, deductively applied is quite commonplace. Researcher known as Katzenstein in 1996 argues that although neo realism holds the promise of a tight, deductive theory, it cannot be directly applied to questions of national security: it is, therefore, employed only as an orienting framework. Many researchers argue that liberalism's propositions cannot be deduced from its assumptions. Few of them suggest that neo realism and neo liberalism are better labelled schools of thought or approaches than theories, neither 'has the integrity' that would enable them to be falsified. Researcher known as Adler in 1997 observes that constructivists seek to explain the social construction of reality, but argues that their reasoning cannot be assimilated to models of deductive proof or inductive generalization. Some explanatory theorists use terms such as 'perspective' in recognition that their theories cannot be deductively applied. For example, researcher known as Keohane in 1989 accepts that liberal institutionalism is a school of thought that provides a perspective on world politics, rather than a 'logically connected deductive theory.

Researcher known as Milner in 1997 acknowledged that the notion of two-level games, on which she draws, may be promising as a framework for analysis but does not constitute a theory with testable hypotheses'. In both cases, a highly significant claim remains implicit and thus unelaborated: that their approaches offer explanatory value even though they cannot be deductively applied. This is the reason why researcher Katzenstein differentiated two meanings of theory in International Relations, general theoretical, orientations, and, research programs. The former provide heuristics, they suggest relevant variables, and, causal patterns that provide guidelines, for developing research programs. The latter link explanatory variables to a set of outcomes, or dependent variables'. Katzenstein et al. describes realism, liberalism, and, constructivism, as general theoretical orientations, but do not specify the connection, between comprehensive orientations, and, research programs. The manner in which these theories contribute to our understanding of international relations, therefore, remains unelaborated.

Neo realism is often represented as generating covering law explanations. This reflects Waltz's account of how to construct a theory of international politics, first, one must conceive of international politics as a bounded realm or domain; second, one must discover some law-like regularity within it; and third, one must develop a way of explaining the observed regularities. However, Waltz also acknowledges the limits of explanatory approaches: he observes that the first immense difficulty lies in finding or stating theories with enough precision and plausibility to make testing worthwhile. He adds that when we have failed to predict, theory still helps us to understand and explain some things about the behaviour of states, implying that neo realism may be useful even without, deductively applied. Waltz's explanation of the absence of direct military confrontation between the superpowers during the Cold War draws on his account of how balancing differs in multi polar, and, bipolar systems. He distinguishes two balancing strategies: 'internal efforts (moves to increase economic capability, to increase military strength, to develop clever strategies) and external efforts (moves to strengthen and enlarge one's own alliance or to weaken and shrink an opposing one)'. He observes, however, that the second strategy is only available in multi Arctic systems, where two powers contend, imbalances can be righted, only by their internal efforts. With more than two, shifts in alignment provide an additional means of adjustment, adding flexibility to the system. Waltz's contention that bipolar systems are relatively stable is peaceful that rests on the lack of flexibility. He overturned the conventional wisdom by arguing that the inflexibility of a bipolar world may promote a greater stability than flexible balances of power among a larger number of states.

If flexibility is to contribute to stability, Waltz argues, it must enable states to change sides in order to tilt the balance against the would-be aggressors, at least one powerful state must overcome the pressure of ideological preference, the pull of former ties, and the conflict of present interests in order to add its weight to the side of the peaceful. Waltz accepts that this may not reliably happen in multi Arctic systems, states may pass the buck, and, a dynamic that associates with the build-up to World War II. Even the states should refrain from free-riding, the timing and content of the actions required to balance against the forces would-be aggressors that become more and more difficult to calculate as the number of extraordinary powers increases. Further, flexibility of alignment may make allies appear unreliable: great powers that depend on their allies for survival may be dragged, to defend those allies, a dynamic Waltz associates with the outbreak of World War I. His point is that uncertainty, arising from flexibility of alignment, amplifies unsettling developments. Rather than making states properly cautious and forwarding the chances of peace, uncertainty and miscalculation cause wars. Prior to the two world wars, he argues, flexibility of alignment made for rigidity of strategy, or, limitation of freedom of decision.

During the Cold War, rigidity of alignment made for flexibility of strategy and the enlargement of freedom of decision. This cannot plausibly be construed as a covering law account. Neo realism's main candidate covering law, which states seeking to survive in anarchic systems engage in balancing behaviour, disproven by Waltz's discussion of the dynamics of multi Arctic systems. The reason is because he fails to specify the circumstances under which states in multi polar systems pass the buck or get locked into chain gangs, Waltz cannot be construed as applying a more specific covering law concerning, when states do or do not balance. Moreover, researcher known as Bueno de Mesquita in 2003 argued that neorealist assumptions imply nothing at all about how uncertainty affects stability. Waltz makes a logical leap from the association of uncertainty with multi polarity to the association of multi polarity with instability and bipolarity with stability. If so, then Waltz's claim that bipolar systems are more dependable than multi Arctic systems is not deductively derived.

Nevertheless, the argument is recognizably neorealist; the theory does perform important heuristic functions. First, it indicates that an explanation should be systemic in form. Waltz presents a structural argument even though this cannot, in the absence of further arguments about the impact of flexibility, resolve the issue. Second, the theory provides organizing concepts, and, Waltz treats categories like superpower and polarity as unproblematic, despite the fact, that during the early Cold War, the USSR was not a superpower and thus the international system was not bipolar, Third, the theory suggests a focus on alliance choices. Waltz emphasizes strategic concerns, downplaying the importance of internal structure. When he considers factors such as ideology, he represents them as working against strategic rationality. However, neo realism's heuristic functions are limited; it offers no insight into alternative responses to the research question fails to problematize its central categories and ignores key mechanisms, conditions and actors. Thus, showing that neo realism is heuristically applied also indicates how it might be improved, what, required is not refinement of its quasi-deductive arguments, but the development of a more critical understanding of the variety of possible explanatory forms, concepts and foci.

Only when neo realism, conceived of as a heuristic resource, it is possible to reconcile Waltz's insistence that it explains a small number of big, and, weighty things, with his acceptance that its explanations are indeterminate, because both unit-level and structural causes are in play. His implicit claim is that any cogent explanation will refer to the structure of the system, but that the way in which structural and, non-structural factors interact cannot be determinately stated. It will vary according to the problem, investigated. This makes it easier to understand why he abstracts from non-structural factors in his theory but refers to them in substantive explanatory claims, as in his acknowledgement that an apparently stable system can always be disrupted by the actions of a Hitler and the reactions of a Chamberlain. His account of the relationship between structural, and, non-structural factors in his discussion of the Cold War international system is specific to that case, and, is not derived from or captured in neo realism's quasi-deductive reasoning. Thus, Waltz in 1997 observed that an explanation is not a theory, what goes into an explanation is not identical with what goes into a theory. This is what researchers would expect if a theory employed as a tool that aids inquiry rather than as a source of deductive explanations.

The idea that explanatory theories in International Relations, typically heuristically applied subverts the idiographic distinction that, often thought to distinguish history from International Relations. According to Levy, for example, historians describe, explain, and interpret individual events, whereas political scientists generalize about the relationship between variables and construct law like statements about social behaviour. Such claims focus on the form in which theories are presented, rather than on how they, actually draw upon in substantive explanations. In International Relations, an explanatory theory's putative causal generalizations are not typically deductively applied. Such theories may be drawn upon as heuristic resources, but historians also require a certain sense for how things work. Moreover, like historians, political scientists often draw on theories' heuristic resources in order to interpret individual events. What distinguishes historians from political scientists who apply explanatory theories heuristically is not the explanatory activity each; engage in, but the form in which they present their sense of how things work. It is, therefore, ironic that form in which explanatory theories, typically presented as quasi-deductive arguments that generate covering laws tends to obscure the explanatory functions that those theories perform.

When a theory is deductively applied, an empirical episode is represented as an instance of a class of such episodes. An explanation is generated by showing that the empirical conditions specified in the theory are fulfilled, but explanatory power resides in the causal generalization under which the episode is subsumed. In contrast, when a theory is heuristically applied, an explanation is generated through empirical or historical inquiry, guided by the theory's heuristic resources. Explanatory power resides in the ensuing account of the episode, not in the theory's quasi-deductive arguments. There is no attempt to show that conditions specified prior to the inquiry are fulfilled. The focus is on developing an account of the episode that provides a persuasive answer to the research question. There are two prerequisites for developing such an account. The first is a theory that provides a clear understanding of the explanation required, useful conceptual categories, and, an appropriate empirical focus. The second is good judgment as to what constitutes a plausible account and judgment plays a key role not only in assessment of competing explanatory claims, but also in their construction.

Ledingham (2003) argued that the "appropriate domain of public relations is, in fact, relationships. The building and sustaining of organization – public relationships requires not only communication, but organizational and public behaviours, a concept central to the relationship management perspective" (p. 194). I also believe that in addition to informing publics, another major role of public relations is to establish and enhance relationships with an organization's publics. This relationship management aspect of public relations is also crucial for the European Union, whose publics have become increasingly sceptical and unaware of the role and goals of this supranational organization.

Public Diplomacy

The need for public diplomacy and reaching out to the foreign publics, in addition to traditional diplomacy practiced by diplomats, became evident in this century. "Public diplomacy, attempting to communicate directly with peoples in other countries, came into its own as an indispensable component of international relations"[14]. Davison (1976) argued that public diplomacy combines the roles of a traditional diplomat, specialist in mass communication and a social researcher. "The diplomat formulates the ideas that he or she would like to have communicated to a foreign public, the social researcher studies the intended audience, and the communications specialist chooses the most appropriate media and composes messages" (p. 399). First understanding, then informing and influencing foreign publics through effective messages is the

[14] Nagy, Zsolt. "Grand Delusions: Interwar Hungarian Cultural Diplomacy, 1918-1941." Order No. 3526146, The University of North Carolina at Chapel Hill, 2012. In PROQUESTMS ProQuest Dissertations & Theses Full Text, http://search.proquest.com/docview/1040729378?accountid=12085.

goal of public diplomacy. How the communication will be perceived by different publics and how messages can be formulated and explained so that they are understood by the foreign publics are important questions public diplomacy strategists have to consider.

Sharp (2007) defined public diplomacy as "the process by which direct relations with people in a country are pursued to advance the interests and extend the values of those being represented" (p. 106). Tuch (1990) also emphasized that publicity and appealing to the public is the purpose of public diplomacy. Zhang (2006) regarded public diplomacy as a process of meaning construction, where states engage in "exchanging symbols, forming and negotiating meanings, and performing acts based on their respective meanings" (p. 27). All of these definitions emphasize that the goal of public diplomacy is trying to explain yourself to foreign publics. Tuch (1990) suggested that public diplomacy, whose goal is to influence attitudes and opinions of foreign publics, requires the use of "modern communications technology as well as such other methods of intercultural communications cultural and educational exchanges, libraries, publications, and people" (p. 10).

The main target audience of public diplomacy is private individuals instead of governments or state officials. In fact, Melissen (2007) stated that the main difference between traditional diplomacy and public diplomacy is the target of the communication efforts.

While traditional diplomacy focuses on "relationships between the representatives of states, or other international actors;" public diplomacy "targets the general public in foreign societies," specifically "non-official groups, organizations and individuals"[15]. But some believe the role of the public's needs to be redefined. Hocking (2007) argued that publics should be seen as active participants in meaning creation, rather than passive objects.

Tuch (1990) also believed that understanding the publics is crucial for the practice of public diplomacy. He believed that this can be achieved through "addressing and communicating with foreign audiences whose history, culture, social processes, and language we must study so that we can project our policies to them in understandable and acceptable ways" (p. 8). Therefore, it is important to see publics as active receivers and to formulate messages and communication strategies according to their needs. This emphasis on publics may be new to the practice of public diplomacy, but it is well accepted among public relations scholars.

Wang (2006) stated that public diplomacy's main goal is to cultivate and manage "a favourable

[15] McGee, Anne E. "Military Soft Power is Not an Oxymoron: Using Public Diplomacy Analytic Approaches to Examine Goals and Effects of U.S. Military Educational Exchange Programs." Order No. 3493881, Georgetown University, 2011. In PROQUESTMS ProQuest Dissertations & Theses Full Text, http://search.proquest.com/docview/920317000?accountid=120 85.

international/world opinion toward a nation-state" (p. 91). However, in today's world, international organizations also need to engage in public diplomacy towards their internal as much as external stakeholders. Stakeholders of an organization are same as its publics; these two terms can be used interchangeably. Stakeholders or publics can be defined as people who might share a common interest with the organization. Using public relations and public diplomacy towards its internal stakeholders, internal publics, is important for the European Union because of its structure that enables it to decide and act as a single unit. The European Union is a major international organization which enables member states to "protect and negotiate their interests, but at the same time, it has the capacity to act in international affairs as a unit"[16].

As states become dependent on each other, human beings become increasingly mobile, and publics gain a say in international decision making, using public diplomacy to communicate about a country to internal and external publics becomes important. As Anholt and Hildreth (2005) argued, public diplomacy has a very important role in communicating a state's culture and policies to international audiences around the world.

[16] Martin, Clifton. "Preventing the Clash: Reexamining U.S. Public Diplomacy in the Middle East." Order No. 1520093, University of Denver, 2012. In PROQUESTMS ProQuest Dissertations & Theses Full Text, http://search.proquest.com/docview/1113390760?accountid=12085.

Public diplomacy has become an important part of a government's international relations and communication efforts for image building, and it consists of a state's communication with international publics to create understanding for its "ideas and ideals, its institutions and culture, as well as its national goals and current policies"[17]. Main instruments of public diplomacy are considered to be: TV, radio broadcasts, films, books, magazines, cultural and educational exchanges, etc. The study will include an analysis of which of these media are being used by the European Union for enhancing immigrant integration and to reach out to the European community.

Parallels between Public Diplomacy and Public Relations

A review of the literature reveals that practices of public relations and public diplomacy share many characteristics. Novoselsky (2007) argued that public diplomacy is more than an interaction between governments. The author argued that the main function of public diplomacy is to build and cultivate relationships, understand "other

---

[17] Litvinsky, Marina. "European Union Public Diplomacy: The Need for a New Frame." Order No. 1477202, The George Washington University, 2010. In PROQUESTMS ProQuest Dissertations & Theses Full Text, http://search.proquest.com/docview/578504400?accountid=120 85.

national and communal needs and identifying areas of shared values and interests" (p. 153). No longer is public diplomacy confined merely to the realm of government relations, but it has evolved to include many different groups of publics.

Leonard (2002) also suggested that public diplomacy's focus should be on building connections between different publics. "Public diplomacy should be about building relationships, starting from understanding other countries' needs, cultures, and peoples and then looking for areas to make common cause" (p. 50). Wang (2007) suggested that public diplomacy's main goal should be to discover commonalities and establish understanding among publics. According to the author, public diplomacy's goal "is not only to promote the policies and values of a particular nation but also to engineer consensus and facilitate understanding among overseas publics" (p. 27). This building connections and establishing understanding between different groups of people is a very important aspect of public diplomacy, something the EU institutions need to utilize to bring together their internal publics. This aspect of public diplomacy reveals its close association with the profession of public relations.

Signitzer and Coombs (1992) claimed that public relations and public diplomacy are becoming similar through a "natural process of convergence" (146). J. Grunig (1993) agreed emphasizing that public diplomacy is actually no more than the "application of public relations to strategic relationship of organizations with international publics" (p. 143). According to J. Grunig (1993), modern governments and international organizations use public relations strategies as part of their public diplomacy strategies; they communicate with foreign publics and with other governments about their culture, policies, ideals, and institutions.

Zhang and Cameron (2003) also argued that public relations and public diplomacy are similar as both practices strive to influence public opinion to benefit their own client or organization. As the authors suggested, public diplomacy, like public relations, tries to influence how others regard a state or an international organization, for example the European Union. Today international or supranational organizations also need to use public relations and public diplomacy to influence publics and increase support their policies, decisions, and actions[18].

Deibel and Roberts (1976) differentiated between tough-minded and tender-minded schools in public diplomacy. The tough-minded diplomacy school holds that "the purpose of diplomacy is to exert and influence on attitudes of foreign audiences

---

[18] Koster, Karleigh. "Pioneers of the Global University: Participant Experience and Study Abroad in Midwestern Public Higher Education from the Cold War to the Present." Order No. 3567291, New York University, 2013. In PROQUESTMS ProQuest Dissertations & Theses Full Text, http://search.proquest.com/docview/1417775979?accountid=12085.

using persuasion and propaganda. Hard political information is considered more important than cultural programs"[19]. Whereas the tender-minded school sees public diplomacy as a cultural function instead of just a method to convey "hard" political information. The authors suggested that "slow media such as films, exhibitions, language instruction, academic and artistic exchanges with a view toward transmitting messages about lifestyles, political and economic systems, and artistic achievements" can be listed as uses of public diplomacy.

While states use public diplomacy, they also make use of public relations strategies. Kunczik (1997) wrote that states use public relations as an image building and reputation management strategy, arguing that for the nation state, PR (public relations) means the planned and continuous distribution of interest-bound information by a state aimed (mostly) at improving the country's image abroad. The author approached public relations efforts of states as persuasive acts of communication produced by a state and directed at foreign audiences, which include the general world public, other governments and international organizations. As Kunczik (1997) argued, states use public relations to build a positive

[19] Keess, John. "Defence, Diplomacy and Discord: The Impact of the Great War and its Effect on Canadian Strategy, 1920--1928." Order No. MR89109, University of New Brunswick (Canada), 2011. In PROQUESTMS ProQuest Dissertations & Theses Full Text, http://search.proquest.com/docview/1153964715?accountid=12085.

reputation in the international arena to project to other states, and this is not much different than public diplomacy.

Public diplomacy and public relations are very similar in the goals they are trying to accomplish. Melissen (2007) suggested that "a lesson that public diplomacy can take on board from the sometimes misunderstood field of PR [public relations] is that the strength of firm relationships largely determines the receipt and success of individual messages and overall attitudes" (p. 21). Importance of cultivating and establishing relationships with the target public is an important area where public diplomacy could learn from the strategies and practices of public relations. In fact, Melissen (2007) even argued that the "US experiences with public diplomacy demonstrate that skills and practices from the corporate sector, in particular from the disciplines of public relations and marketing, can be particularly useful in public diplomacy campaigns" (p. 8).

Public relations are getting integrated into the foreign policies of states as they get heavily dependent on how they are perceived and their reputations in the international arena. Wang and Chang (2004) also emphasized the importance of public relations activities of states for creating and maintaining a positive public opinion. "With the revolution in modern communication technologies and the rapid globalization of international politics and economy, governments increasingly come to appreciate the important role such public relations events play in cultivating and mobilizing international public opinion support" (p. 11).

Communitarianism, Community Relations, and Nation Building

Communitarianism is a public relations approach that is also closely related to the topic of this study. communitarianism supports the idea that individuals and organizations are responsible to others and the community and it should be used for guiding public relations practices. Because in the end, what is best for the community is ultimately in the best interest of the organization[20]. Kruckeberg and Starck (1988) supported a communitarian approach to public relations. In an extensively quoted statement, the authors expressed that "public relations is better defined and practiced as the active attempt to restore and maintain a sense of community" (p. xi). Leeper (1996) also argued that communitarianism is important for public relations practice and regarded communitarianism as an ethical base for public relations, where the main goal of public relations becomes establishing and supporting a sense of community.

---

[20] Gu, Yao. "Byron's "Don Juan" and Nationalism." Order No. 3436617, The Chinese University of Hong Kong (Hong Kong), 2010. In PROQUESTMS ProQuest Dissertations & Theses Full Text, http://search.proquest.com/docview/822408732?accountid=120 85.

A community-building approach to public relations aims to bring together people around common interests and values. Community building is also related to the goal of the European Union, which is to inform people and unite them around a common European identity. Immigrant integration also falls under community building. As Hallahan (2004) suggested, community building aims to integrate people and organizations around "a functional collectivity that strives toward common or compatible goals" (p. 259). European Union public relations and public diplomacy efforts for immigrant integration may be seen as part of this community-building approach. Hallahan (2004) listed the three community-building activities as community involvement, community nurturing, and community organizing. Community involvement starts with managing and enhancing an organization's reputation among the members of the community. Community nurturing involves improving the political, economic, and socio-cultural aspects of communities through support systems, special events, and distributing information. Immigrant integration also falls under community nurturing. The last aspect, community organizing, happens when public relations strategies are utilized to improve economic and social conditions, especially for specific groups, i.e. immigrant groups.

Another approach used in public relations, which is very similar to what public diplomacy tries to accomplish is nation building. A nation-building approach to public relations and communication is concerned with how to create a national identity and unity. The EU efforts to create a common European identity across EU member states can fall under nation building even though the identity being created is not a national, but a regional (European) one. Is this possible? Could there be a common, EU-wide, transnational European identity accepted by all EU citizens despite the national differences between the member states? Even though this is a strongly debated issue, Jolly (2005) argued that having an ethno-cultural dimension is not a prerequisite for creating a common identity and transnational solidarity. Thus having shared civic values might be enough to bring the European population, including the immigrant, together through commitment to "democracy, liberty, tolerance, to social models of political economy, including the respect of, and even, appreciation of diversity" (p. 16).

Communication, through public relations and public diplomacy efforts, may help foster integration and the creation of a collective European identity. This is one of the goals of the European Union as it promotes the formation of a common European identity around shared interests, a common consciousness, and unity[21]. Nation building is

[21] Froh, David. "Soft Power, Constructivism and the Rwandan Genocide." Order No. MR88566, The University of Regina (Canada), 2010. In PROQUESTMS ProQuest Dissertations & Theses Full Text, http://search.proquest.com/docview/1064955196?accountid=12085.

another approach to public relations which may be helpful in explaining the EU efforts to establish a common identity. Although this European identity is not exactly national but an EU-wide one, the nation building scholarship can still be applied to this situation. Nation building can be referred to as an application of relationship building, where, as Taylor and Kent (2006) suggested, "conditions under which people of various ethnic groups can be mobilized to cooperate with each other" is the goal (p. 356).

Taylor and Kent (2006) suggested that communication and public relations is a major part of nation building as it enhances relationships among individuals. A public relations approach to nation building uses "a more elaborate model of communication that focuses on how meanings are socially constructed" (p. 346). The European Union tries to do the same through EU-wide strategies to create a common European identity. This study hopes to explain how the nation-building approach to public relations is being used in EU public relations and public diplomacy efforts to enhance community building and to establish a common European identity through nation building.

European Union, Public Diplomacy, and Public Relations

In the past, public diplomacy was seen as a tool for communicating with foreign publics and it was used solely by diplomats. The world was a

different   place   then.   The   increased
interconnectedness   of   people   and   the   shifting
relationship between foreign versus domestic publics
due to globalization and developed communication
technologies changed the world[22]. Today, the
definition of public diplomacy, which had been
traditionally seen as communication and other
activities targeted at foreign publics, needs to be
reconsidered due to the interconnectedness of foreign
and domestic audiences. As Melissen (2007) argued,
the relationship between public relations and public
diplomacy has become intricate, "separating public
affairs (aimed at domestic audiences) from public
diplomacy (dealing with overseas target groups) is
increasingly at odds with the 'interconnected'
realities of global relationships" (p. 13).

The rise of public diplomacy as a soft power
targeted at communicating with ordinary people
rather diplomats is a necessity of the globalized
world with its vast information and communication
technologies. Ordinary citizens become the new
receivers of public diplomacy messages rather than
diplomats. The new public diplomacy is seen as a
"two-way street," where there is "persuasion by

---

[22] Diawara, Marieme A. "Islam and Public Health: French
Management of the Hajj from Colonial Senegal and Muslim
Responses Beginning in 1895." Order No. 3504135, Michigan
State University, 2012. In PROQUESTMS ProQuest
Dissertations & Theses Full Text,
http://search.proquest.com/docview/1010783877?accountid=12
085.

means of dialogue" and it is important to "listen to what people have to say" (p. 18).

Gilboa (2008) stated that research on public diplomacy has been mostly limited to the study of countries, mostly the United States, while public diplomacy efforts of NGOs, civil society groups, and individuals have mostly been ignored. Therefore, Gilboa (2008) suggested that three areas should be given special attention in public diplomacy research including: The Internet, NGOs, and evaluation of public diplomacy. The study of how large international organizations use public diplomacy is important to develop new ways of looking at public diplomacy and to increase the areas where it can be used to communicate with people and establish relationships.

The European Union is gaining power in the international arena as a large decision maker consisting of 27 member states. Brown and Studemeister (2003) suggested that there is a global trend toward powerful nongovernmental organizations, international social movements, and transnational networks that have growing international decision making power. The growing European Union is also influenced by this trend. Melissen (2007) also argued that public diplomacy is not limited to states or governments and provided the European Commission as an example of giving priority to developing communication strategies for the European Union and trying to develop an EU public diplomacy strategy. "Large and small non-state actors, and supranational and subnational players develop public diplomacy policies of their own." (p. 12).

Although public diplomacy is mostly used by states, the European Union also needs to use public diplomacy and public relations. The European Union is a powerful international organization or a supranational organization as some would suggest, some policies get produced within the institutions of the EU and are transmitted to the international agenda independently of the will of the states that created the organization. However, although the European Union has the capacity to act as a unit, due to its structure the implementation of some EU level decisions and initiatives are left at the discretion of the member states, since national implementation of EU policies are controlled by the member states[23].

As countries get more interconnected, the need for public diplomacy increases. As Melissen (2007) argued, public diplomacy has become an essential tool for highly interdependent areas and between countries that have become interconnected due to transnational economic or political relationships. This interdependence and

---

[23] Cheng, Zhuqing. "An Examination of the First- and Second-Level of Agenda Building with the Image of China's President Xi Jinping in Xinhua and Four U.S. News Outlets." Order No. 1564859, Syracuse University, 2014. In PROQUESTMS ProQuest Dissertations & Theses Full Text, http://search.proquest.com/docview/1615884246?accountid=12085.

interconnectedness of countries has also resulted in the interconnectedness of the civil societies, of the people living in these countries, which is a characteristic of the European Union. In fact, EU citizenship has created a common civil society among the peoples of different European countries. Michalski (2007) stressed that a unique quality of EU's public diplomacy is that it is practiced at two levels, first addressing European domestic audiences, meaning citizens and residents, and also targeting audiences who live outside of EU borders. As a large supranational entity, the EU public diplomatic efforts, it communication with EU citizens and residents and also with the rest of the world should be studied in order to understand the importance of public diplomacy for such a large international organization and to develop ways of improving its communication with its publics.

Michalski (2007) argued that developing EU public diplomacy strategies for EU citizens and residents is especially important for the EU institutions. In fact, "(f)aced with an increasingly sceptical public, the Commission has realized that it needs to justify its actions and policies in the area of external relations with the populations of the member states, as well as with publics in third countries, in order to build a positive public image, promote European values and ultimately enhance the EU's legitimacy" (p. 143). On the other hand, Michalski (2007) also highlighted the fact that the research he conducted with EU officials revealed that the concept of public diplomacy is not employed, not even recognized, among the majority of officials. In addition this term was not used in any Commission or Council Secretariat policy papers or other types of EU communication.

However, although the term is not used exclusively, EU actions and strategies to inform external and internal publics fit within the framework of public diplomacy. The Commission acknowledges the importance of explaining policies and actions to the internal and external EU publics. The Commission recognizes that it has only weak instruments to influence national public opinion and is therefore dependent on existing national channels and opinion formers[24]. In order to do so, the EU Commission emphasizes encouraging "dialogue with civil society within as well as outside the EU through a variety of different kinds of links and networks. They can take the shape of interest based networks with groups that have a direct stake in a policy (such as the environment, social rights, trade, or humanitarian aid), with which the Commission interacts in a two-way communication process" (Michalski, 2007, p. 139). The goal is to encourage support and inform publics about the European Union, in addition to developing relationships with

---

[24] Budabin, Alexandra Cosima. "Citizens' Army for Darfur the Impact of a Social Movement on International Conflict Resolution." Order No. 3495816, New School University, 2012. In PROQUESTMS ProQuest Dissertations & Theses Full Text, http://search.proquest.com/docview/924490309?accountid=120 85.

civil society organizations and non governmental bodies in addition to individuals.

The European Union needs to use public relations and public diplomacy to establish a positive public opinion among all of its publics, including internal publics. These internal EU publics include EU citizens and permanent residents of EU member states, who are very important as these populations make-up the public opinion and may influence EU decision making or influence policy implementation in their respective states. As the European Union gains more power, the need to keep EU citizens informed increases and the need to integrate citizens and residents, especially immigrants, becomes important for community building within the enlarging European Union.

Therefore, public diplomacy is needed by the EU institutions to influence decision making, policy adoption, and implementation by member states. In addition, public relations and public diplomacy are needed to influence the perception of these EU member state citizens. Miller and Schlesinger (2001) emphasized the importance of lobbying and public relations activities for the EU member states, arguing that these activities need to be diversified since they do not only target "the EU institutions (although that is their primary arena) but also national and regional governments in the member states" (p. 682).

The European Union utilizes public relations and public diplomacy because it needs to manage relationships between its member states and with its publics. As Scott-Smith (2005) suggested, "the EU is fundamentally committed to achieving trans-national consensus based upon the mutual acceptance of rules and procedures" by the member states and their citizens (p. 749). The European Union needs to utilize public relations and public diplomacy strategies not just abroad, but also within its own borders to increase support among EU citizens and residents about the union and to enhance the integration of EU citizens and residents, especially the immigrants. This is also crucial for community building at the European Union level, which is crucial for the creation of a common European identity[25].

Community building is another important function of public diplomacy. Ledingham (2001) explored how public relations, as part of public diplomacy efforts, can contribute to community building by nurturing relationships and bringing together diverse populations through reducing conflict, and by resolving differences and conflicting perceptions. For the European Union, utilizing public diplomacy for its diverse publics is important to create a common ground to negotiate meanings, improve EU reputation, and nurture relationships between different communities within its borders.

[25] Blaustein, George Holt, Jr. "To the Heart of Europe: Americanism, the Salzburg Seminar, and Cultural Diplomacy." Order No. 3395409, Harvard University, 2010. In PROQUESTMS ProQuest Dissertations & Theses Full Text, http://search.proquest.com/docview/305213248?accountid=120 85.

Utilizing public relations and public diplomacy to integrate its increasingly diverse population, especially immigrants living in Europe, should be a major goal for the European Union to reduce conflict and enhance community building.

The European Union also needs to use public relations and public diplomacy to promote its founding principles, which include: Democracy, human rights, and the rule of law among its internal and external publics. The European Union tries to express these values in most of its internal and external communication activities. Petiteville (2003) referred to the communication of these values and principles as soft diplomacy, which he defined as "diplomacy resorting to economic, financial, legal, and institutional means to export values, norms and rules and achieve long-term cultural influence" (p. 134).

Although it is complicated to design and implement, a common EU public diplomacy strategy is needed. As Lynch (2005) suggested, a common EU public diplomacy strategy needs to combine member state and EU efforts. "It is difficult enough for a single state to design effective public diplomacy; the challenge for a union of 25 [as of the publication's date] states is daunting" (p. 22). European Union is seen as distant, impersonal, and operates in twenty [as of the publication's date] official languages; there is no European 'people,' only European 'peoples'; there is no common language or media. All of these make communicating

to the EU publics, including the European civil
society, a major challenge for the EU institutions.

An important point about European Union's
public diplomatic efforts Michalski (2007) made is
that although the term public diplomacy is not used
in official Commission or Council documents, public
diplomacy is utilized during external and internal
communication when trying to persuade audiences
about policies and actions and communicate with
different groups in civil society. Communication of
policy initiatives is taken seriously by the European
Union. As Michalski (2007) stated, the European
Commission focuses on "the communication
dimension at an early stage of the elaboration of
policy initiatives" (p. 134). The European Union,
specifically the European Commission, recognizes
that communicating with European citizens and
residents living in the member states "is the weak
element of the Commission's strategy and realizes
that the 'fact-and-figures' approach that prevailed in
the past is not the appropriate way to carry out public
communication" (p. 135). Instead, the Commission's
goal is to communicate "people-focused 'success
stories' to the European public," and explain EU
legislation, policies and action in all areas.

In fact, Valentini (2007) stated that the
European Union now opts for a new approach in its
public diplomatic efforts and communicates "'with'
and not 'to' Europeans" (p. 119). Thus, developing
understanding and forming relationships becomes the
main goal. Public relations and public diplomacy

intertwine as the focus becomes the establishment of firm relationships that determine the receipt and success of individual messages and overall attitudes.

Managing relationship with different people who come from different national and cultural backgrounds is the challenge the European Union faces today. Community building is an important part of what the European Union needs to do through its public relations and public diplomacy efforts in order to create a common European identity[26]. Incorporating public relations strategies and trying to establish two-way communication is an important step that the EU needs to take to reach its goal. Public relationship management in different national cultural contexts, like those within the European Union, should be culturally oriented and based on a two-way symmetrical flow of communication and on community-building relationships. However, this is easier said than done as the European Union rarely communicates with its citizens and residents directly.

A major hindrance the European Union faces when trying to communicate with its publics is that EU messages are communicated through national media, where the messages become "nationalized"

---

[26] Abdel Samei, Marwa. "Public Diplomacy in the Age of Regional Media: Winning the War of Hearts and Minds in the Middle East AL-Jazeera and Al-Hurra." Order No. 3411814, Northeastern University, 2010. In PROQUESTMS ProQuest Dissertations & Theses Full Text, http://search.proquest.com/docview/649191171?accountid=120 85.

by the member states "to fit the domestic arena". EU messages get to be reproduced through a domestic perspective, which causes the reinforcement of sentiment of competition or conflict rather than cooperation and longer-term commitment. Therefore, EU-level communication, without the interference of national media and perspectives, is really important because it will ensure that the messages will be clear of national prejudices and be able to reach European citizens and residents as intended.

A way to ensure open communication with the European public is to engage in dialogue with civil society. Michalski (2007) suggested that this can be done by establishing networks and engaging in two-way communication with interest groups, such as citizens' or civil rights, that can be influenced by a policy. Interacting with interest groups may be helpful for the European Union while developing new policies and also trying to inform the public about them during their implementation[27].

This is where the research question of this study becomes relevant. Does the European Union engage in this kind of two-way relationship, in a dialogue with special interest or civil rights groups

---

[27] Chahhou, Khalid. "The Status of Languages in Post-Independent Morocco: Moroccan National Policies and Spanish Cultural Action." Order No. 3641830, City University of New York, 2014. In PROQUESTMS ProQuest Dissertations & Theses Full Text, http://search.proquest.com/docview/1623001438?accountid=12085.

when developing and communicating a new action or a policy? More specifically, how does the European Union communicate its immigrant integration decisions and initiatives to EU citizens and residents? Is there any direct relationship with immigrant or ethnic minority groups and their associations? Can these immigrant organizations have any influence or say in EU-level immigrant integration decisions and initiatives; is there any active lobbying or other type of persuasive strategies among immigrant groups?

Valentini (2007) argued that EU public relations and public diplomacy efforts should be tailored for "community's needs and for a cooperative approach with their publics" (p. 124). This study tries to find out whether the European Union tailors its communication efforts and cooperates with its various publics, specifically focusing on Turkish immigrant associations living in the heart of the European Union, in Brussels. Valentini (2007) stressed those international organizations, such as the European Union, "know that in order to induce specific behavioural changes in situations of high involvement, they need to communicate with the language, the values and norms of their publics" (p. 123).

The Media Sphere

Media set of non-state actors are increasingly being seen as taking the role of government: to inform their citizens. This is especially true in developing countries where the media used to be the exclusive prerogative of the state. Again, the role of the media in relation to state sovereignty is disputed among scholars of international relations. With the advances in media technology, some argue that while the media used to be an average of the nation-state to convince citizens through the promotion of national identity and interest, is currently under the influence of local and international factors. Price for Monroe, "The changing nature of media sphere in the nation-states has brought new challenges to national images of identity produced by the state and led to the emergence of new points to represent the identity." Other scholars argue that the state still has the ability and the means by which it protects its information space and, therefore, maintains its national identity. Examples of this can go from the states that control the Internet within its borders - for example, China and Iraq under Saddam Hussein, and want to have indirect control over satellite reception by the requirement called "rising" which means any information or images that are sent from the satellite people within the borders of the state should be transferred from its territory. Those who see the growing influence of the media consider the element / effective drug fall of the Berlin Wall[28].

The article proponents argue that media images of Western society, especially coming from

[28] Kinstetter, Gregory A. "Let Poland be Poland." Order No. 1510007, University of Wyoming, 2012. In PROQUESTMS ProQuest Dissertations & Theses Full Text, http://search.proquest.com/docview/1015032502?accountid=12 085.

these ads are responsible, to some extent, the fall of the Berlin Wall and the collapse of the Soviet Union. They argue that the same thing can be done in the spread of democratic values throughout the world. Such a statement is sometimes, from the point of view of developing countries as a threat to national identity, especially with the spread of satellite television and other cultural content they introduce. In societies, theses, reducing dependence on public broadcasting and the impact of foreign media content (e.g., advertisements) are cultural and political significance. People see on TV different lifestyle to which they aspire, regardless of their economic reality. This export of western consumer culture is seen as an obstacle to development and economic growth. Thus, economic and cultural factors of vulnerability are closely related as free trade and economic growth, as they say, is impossible without information on free trade. In addition, it is   assumed that the use of information technologies have an impact on self-image, poor developing countries[29].

Gareth Locksley refers to information technology as "e-colonialism." It is primarily concerned with the image of the developing countries in the news North / West, tend to portray these areas riddled with earthquakes and natural and environmental disasters. He argues that the

[29] Hall, Christa Marie. "Peace Corps to the Right: An Analysis of the U.S. Peace Corps in Central America." Order No. 1491414, Georgetown University, 2011. In PROQUESTMS ProQuest Dissertations & Theses Full Text, http://search.proquest.com/docview/865808684?accountid=120 85.

restructuring of the international information technology relations in accordance with the ownership of information. The power relations, therefore, rely on information and consolidation of those who control it. This is achieved by promoting the ideology of the free flow of information and the idea that the market offers the best mechanisms for the creation and dissemination of information and culture. Thus, information society based class society is a serious threat to the developing countries.

There is another aspect of the media role in different countries which affects the relationship between cultures and civilizations. This was the case after the end of the Cold War. Some analysts argue that the reason why the concept of a "clash of civilizations," Huntington received such treatment in the media is the fact that helped shape the media attention on the coverage of world news. Moving to the uncertainty in the cold post-war era without much sense as the new world order emerging, says Philip Seib, the media "were receptive to new geopolitical schemes, especially the one who told identifiable adverse relationship to replace those who have left behind"[30].

---

[30] Ginzburg, Lyubov. "Confronting the Cold War Legacy: The Forgotten History of the American Colony in St Petersburg a Case Study of Reconciliation." Order No. 3409068, University of Kansas, 2010. In PROQUESTMS ProQuest Dissertations & Theses Full Text, http://search.proquest.com/docview/612741904?accountid=120 85.

Foreign editor of The New York Times Bernard sent a memo to his staff in December 1992, calls for adjustments in coverage: "In the old days, when some countries were pawns in the Cold War, its political orientation alone was reason enough to cover them. Now, with its political orientation is not as important as we do not want to forget about them, but we have the opportunity to explore different aspects of the full community. It sheds light on the development of relations between the perceived media and hegemony. While much of the discussion was this relationship in a society, we can talk about it in different countries. At the national level, some scholars argue that the media reflect the culture of the dominant group and serve their interests.

Italian thinker developed a term for moral and cultural leadership, which led him to be a prerequisite for any class that is committed to social control. Gramsci's idea is directly related to national identity. To use the words of Gramsci, these "organic intellectuals" have a big impact on what to emphasize contempt or invent under the hegemony of national identity in a way that legitimizes the existing social order. In the present era, the media role has become questionable due to the changing nature of information technology and communications. It means that the media have become tools in the community to maintain the distribution of power among which are dominant, contributing to a set of political views and cultural ideas and slogans that help maintain the existing structure of power. New developments in the media, according to Monroe, challenged this provision[31].

The government, in this context, there are two strategies to respond. One revises the cartel and useful new participants, and the second takes effective measures (by law or by the use of force) to try and raise barriers to entry. This view can be applied to the international arena. Lifting the barriers to entry in fact what happened at the international level in general and in the Arab world in particular. International media were predominantly Western in terms of possession and points of view that raises concerns as to its impact on national culture and identity. However, in the 1990s, considered the turning point for many countries, especially in the Arab world. Philip Seib claimed the war in the Persian Gulf this year [1990] in many ways the last gasp of Western hegemony connection. The slogan of CNN, at the time was: "The world is watching CNN." This was true because most of the world does not have much choice.

For CNN and other information providers in America and Europe almost void in the global mass news, entertainment, and other information products that may have a global reach, but not a cultural domination can be immortalized in a limited system;

[31] Fouladvand, Hida. "Public Diplomacy Gangnam Style." Order No. 1556438, Georgetown University, 2014. In PROQUESTMS ProQuest Dissertations & Theses Full Text, http://search.proquest.com/docview/1539537560?accountid=12085.

other voices have not been heard. Global television, such as CNN, has created new phenomenon media event live historical events around the world. Pierre Robinson argues that this new type of lighting was to influence the foreign policy throughout the world, an effect that became known as the "CNN effect". The important result of CNN, however, that the poor performance of the national media, especially in companies controlled by the media showed[32].

It was strongly felt in the Arab world, as described below. What is important to the emergence of Al Jazeera in the Arab world. Al-Jazeera, in many respects, a challenge Western hegemony in the production of news. He became a new model of media that Seib described as "al-Jazeera effect". Bazovaya station in Qatar, played a historic role in the transformation of the media not only in the Middle East, but also on a global scale, demonstrating that the hegemony of the predominantly Western establishment media can be challenged successfully, in addition to Al-Jazeera's own success in this regard, the channel serves as a model in the Arab world and beyond, and the example of news organizations regional and global levels, where it is undoubtedly grow in the next decade. Thus, the media play an important role in

---

[32] Eibl, Marita. "PEPFAR, Politics, and Patients / Antiretroviral Treatment in Tanzania." Order No. 3435232, Michigan State University, 2010. In PROQUESTMS ProQuest Dissertations & Theses Full Text,
http://search.proquest.com/docview/816030283?accountid=120 85.

world politics. May facilitate the contacts or cause a conflict through its interpretation of the image.

Benedict Anderson argues, any nation "itself a political community" when he takes a "deep, horizontal comradeship" in a way that makes people willing to die for him. According to Seib, new communication technologies and the media can play an important role in creating an imagined community in imaginary boundaries. This shows how "The government lost the monopoly they used to enjoy more of certain types of information, and therefore have fewer opportunities for direct political [and international] economy[33].

Traditional instruments ministries of information and promotion of state censorship wilting, and the government must create new strategies and tools to cope with the new environment. "The role of non-state actors, therefore, challenged the national identity of the state as a very complex external influences version of identity of the state and contributes to others. Advances in communications and information played an important role in this context, and there was a general factor that has received attention from various approaches in international relations as a new

[33] Donos, Maxim. "Communicating Sport Mega-Events and the Soft Power Dimensions of Public Diplomacy." Order No. MR86488, University of Ottawa (Canada), 2012. In PROQUESTMS ProQuest Dissertations & Theses Full Text, http://search.proquest.com/docview/1356818844?accountid=12085.

threat to cultivate the ability of the national state identity national particularly among its citizens. Globalization creates an identity crisis for many countries. On the one hand, people receive foreign cultural products such as films, novels, music and news competing "national" media information and the dominant culture.

The Modern Diplomatic Environment

For the most of the twentieth century, the state and its customary diplomatic institution were the essential conductor for most matters global. Notwithstanding, a depiction of the cutting edge diplomatic environment recommends a more diffuse scene. What's more, this depiction uncovers the impediments inborn to the customary, statist method for deduction and expounding on diplomacy. In the advanced diplomatic environment the state is the most predominant political performing artist while its diplomatic institution (midway organized by the Ministry of Foreign Affairs) remains the most obvious diplomatic performer. In the physical sense, customary diplomacy has "turn into a development area" and remains the "motor room of global relations"[34]. As of now, there are 191 states working in the current diplomatic environment, contrasted

[34] Choi, Suh Hee. "Conceptualizing Tourism Image and Nation Image: An Integrated Relational-Behavioral Model." Order No. 3507221, Purdue University, 2011. In PROQUESTMS ProQuest Dissertations & Theses Full Text, http://search.proquest.com/docview/1015364634?accountid=12085.

with 47 in 1950 and 26 in 1926. All of these states cooperates diplomatically, all need to speak to themselves, and all need constantly to arrange worthwhile remote strategy closes in a focused and every so often antagonistic environment. With in excess of three hundred years of related experience, the remote consulate persists as the main diplomatic performer, where "the behaviour of relations on a state-to-state premise, by means of formally authorize inhabitant missions structures the majority of worldwide trade.

Along these lines, a conventional methodology to composing and pondering diplomacy should not be surrendered. This methodology, with a stress on the state and its diplomacy, is pervasive, profitable, and essential for the diplomacy studies field. Also regarding one performer the state—it is both sufficient and catholic. Be that as it may all is not well in the customary patio. Notwithstanding perpetually tightening plan and contracting quantities of abroad missions and staff, the re-examination of the traditional diplomatic institution is clear. Presently these institutions need to advocate their importance to a more educated household crowd. This avocation incorporates two-way correspondence forms with local and worldwide publics (rather than the conventional restricted techniques which strengthened the hermetic picture of numerous institutions); the incorporation of numerous non state specialists into the consecrated corridors of diplomacy; and the shift in recruitment approaches to construct staffs positively intelligent of the household societal strata they imply to speak to, to name however a couple of changes. This depiction recommends that the conventional "watchmen" are attempting to keep up pertinence and are transforming in an offer to hold tight to the keys to the entryway[35].

On the opposite side of the door, energized, progressively proficient, and various non state on-screen characters are social occasion. There is a relationship between their climbing numbers and developing impact. Case in point, the quantity of NGOs has climbed from 997 in 1954 to 20,928 in 2005/ 2006. The substantial quantities of MNCs are likewise critical. Toward the start of the twenty-first century there are more than 53,000 MNCs, which have in excess of 450,000 remote associates. These constantly developing numbers propose that MNCs exercise critical clout in the cutting edge diplomatic framework, with worldwide resources in abundance of $13 trillion (USD) and worldwide offers of more than $9.5 trillion (USD). Also more than a large portion of the world's top economies are not nations however worldwide MNCs, with winding down affiliations to the country state. The development of NGOs in the most recent hundred years is

[35] Butts, Robert H. "An Architect of the American Century: Colonel Edward M. House and the Modernization of United States Diplomacy." Order No. 3443311, Texas Christian University, 2010. In PROQUESTMS ProQuest Dissertations & Theses Full Text, http://search.proquest.com/docview/854839987?accountid=120 85.

additionally huge. In 1909, there were 37 NGOs, by 1962 this number had climbed to 163, and by 2005/2006 the present day diplomatic environment had 1,963 NGOs. To delegates from this developing non state area, the entryway no more looks so forcing o? outright; there are numerous different ways around the side.

In the present day diplomatic environment, these non state gatherings have embraced essential diplomatic capacities, for example, arrangement aptitudes, noticeable representation, successful correspondence, sifted data, and political reporting from abroad and imagery (the Greenpeace rainbow banner is immediately conspicuous, as are the pervasive brilliant curves). Huge MNCs, as one case, are learning of the need to create their undertaking characterized diplomatic structures to serve their specific needs and create nearby mastery that national diplomatic administrations discover hard to adversary'. Where before there was one way and one entryway there are currently numerous channels, systems and exchange environments through which to take part in diplomacy.

Bunch examples of hilter kilter and polylateral diplomacy are seeming, including state delegates as well as agents from NGOs, transnational associations (the External Delegations of the European Union, for instance), and even renowned however barely viable motion picture stars. The Ottawa Process, the Kimberley Diamonds Process, or the Nazi Gold settlement—examples of overcoming adversity of ""capricious"" diplomacy—are frequently trumpeted and are utilized as proof to recommend the introducing of a period of ""new"" diplomacy (once more!)[36].

Whether it is multi-lateralism or summitry or two people from distinctive nations chatting on a plane, diplomacy is blooming and unmistakably no more aphoristically connected to the state. Conventional written work on diplomacy just tells piece of this cutting edge diplomatic story. It sufficiently represents the chronicled and current part of the state in diplomacy however neglects to clarify the multiplication and effect of unpredictable, "new" diplomatic performing artists. A look at the ordinance of diplomacy studies proposes that the conventional method for contemplating diplomacy is generally challenged.

Beyond Modern Diplomacy

Seeing diplomacy in representational terms gives a wealthier understanding of what diplomats do than does the ordinary record of it as "one of the lesser apparatuses of outside strategy. The diplomats of the cutting edge state framework guaranteed that

[36] Aden, Ubah A. "The Birth of Post-War U.S. Government Propaganda: The Truman Administration and its Ideological Struggle with the Union of Soviet Socialist Republics (USSR)." Order No. 1509516, Georgetown University, 2012. In PROQUESTMS ProQuest Dissertations & Theses Full Text, http://search.proquest.com/docview/1013827223?accountid=12 085.

nobody else possessed the position of separation from the worldwide society of states, or performed the part of speaking to its parts to the world and the world again to them. Presently, it is getting to be progressively conceivable to claim that more individuals are so utilized and more are "diplomats." A clear expansion of the methodology of review diplomacy as representation is to apply it to the "new" diplomatic performing artists of contemporary universal relations[37].

An evident desire of the methodology laid out above is that the new diplomats, in the same way as the diplomats of progressive administrations before them, will do much modifying. Their capacity to realize change in the expert and political universes of diplomacy will be restricted. This is not a contention in any straightforward feeling of that term. New on-screen characters don't need to comply with the principles of the amusement as it is played by old actors (read rich and capable) on the grounds that that is the thing that the old ones need. rather, it is the agents of performers for whom solidarity, independence, and personality stay imperative. They confront comparable dilemmas, whether they speak to the old or new, the rich or poor, the solid or feeble. All face the issue of helping the creation and

---

[37] Colona,William T.,,II. "Social Media and the Advancement of America's Soft Power by Public Diplomacy." Order No. 1508114, Georgetown University, 2012. In PROQUESTMS ProQuest Dissertations & Theses Full Text, http://search.proquest.com/docview/968947391?accountid=120 85.

multiplication of the personalities they speak to in, and by, their relations with each other. Different diversions financial, military, political, and social— are going on as well, however their importance differs by performer, arrangement, and connection, representation, as effectively examined, is regular to all performers in universal relations and is specific to it[38]. This is not as large a case as it may sound. The inquiry of whether new diplomatic on-screen characters acknowledge the political and expert universes of diplomacy recognizes that they likewise work in a more extensive universe of worldwide thought and activity in which these different performing artists attempt to capacity with their own particular universes and related operational codes. Consider two built ideas, sway and country. Both show up as conspicuous blocks in the structure of diplomacy's expert and political planets, yet both likewise fit in with different planets where the systemic and directing distractions of diplomacy appear to have almost no spot.

Notwithstanding how diplomacy tames, oversees, and utilizes these two thoughts for itself, it is worth looking at how diplomacy adapts when others have distinctive originations and needs. As James Mayall notes, diplomacy was one of the few global institutions to survive the invasion of

[38] Dougherty, Jill. "Russia's "Soft Power" Strategy." Order No. 1556260, Georgetown University, 2013. In PROQUESTMS ProQuest Dissertations & Theses Full Text, http://search.proquest.com/docview/1540812881?accountid=12 085.

mainstream power and nineteenth-century patriotism. Mayall's diplomacy, and about everybody else's, is the diplomacy of the cutting edge regional state, with a viable and obviously identifiable sovereign site. We underestimate this so much that we may solicit whether diplomacy in the nonattendance from sovereigns may be legitimately termed "diplomacy." Instead, we may ask, How did diplomacy survive modernity's Clearly the answer is adjustment. By what means will diplomacy survive experiences with ideas past which it has generally not asserted, for example, race, class, sex, and developments (not Civilization) It is past my ability to talk about these thoughts, other than to note that even at routine meetings on diplomacy, papers on issues like "the issue of mates and partners are frequently exhibited.

Discomforting however these methodologies are to a portion of the members, not these topics or the universes of contentions and suspicions about social life from which they stem will go away. Creating a successful diplomatic mission today includes tending to patriarchy and character issues, and also the issues postured for security and institutional memory by electronic mailing frameworks. The investigation of diplomacy and what diplomats need to say in regards to it will claim not to structuralisms or to constructivists in their individual solid structures. Diplomacy presumes that structures don't clarify all results, or even simply the paramount ones, yet it likewise considers existing structures important. Structures may be constituted by the act of specialists. In recognizing this, diplomats are unrealistic to surrender that we have adapted much about the probability of specific structures clinging, advancing, or caving in regardless of the fact that their own particular nature is to wager on adhering.

Outcomes of Diplomatic Interaction

The outcomes of diplomatic connection in the middle of governments differ colossally, essentially as per how compelling the specific state is, and secondarily as per whether the NSEE is a MEI that holds substantial tote strings on which an administration may depend. Feeble states and creating nations are frequently in the position of supplicant, for example, the IMF, World Bank and provincial advancement banks, whose agents regularly wield incredible control over creating nations' local economies[39]. As far as force relations and going with diplomatic practice, legislatures of states perspective Meis not as an issue government, so the relationship is not that of U.s. states or German Länder managing their separate Federal Governments. Nor can anymore be seen as consistently subordinate bodies to country state governments, so a Federal Government to U.s. state or German Land similarity, in which regulatory

[39] Elliot, Daniel J. "Exploring the Relationship between Educational Inequality and Group-Level Armed Conflict within a Country." Order No. 1554554, Georgetown University, 2014. In PROQUESTMS ProQuest Dissertations & Theses Full Text, http://search.proquest.com/docview/1528531200?accountid=12085.

contemplations may have a tendency to prevail over the political, would be just as off the imprint.

these are liable to view governments as indicated by whether the legislature is a net supplier or beneficiary of the institution's trusts. A finer relationship for NSEE-government connection would be the way that country state governments respect different governments: each one matching of governments will reflect an alternate dispersion of force, both social and structural, between them, an alternate authentic and social foundation to the relationship, an alternate institutional development of the relationship. Consequently diplomacy between country state governments, considered as an issue, and considered as an issue, is prone to vary regarding force conveyance, institutional similarity, and other important variables similarly that diplomacy as generally imagined between country state governments shifts.

An understanding of how diplomatic communications in the middle and governments deciphers into results obliges drawing upon the scope of speculations of force from the International relations/International Political Economy writing. Hypothetical methodologies, for example, Neoliberalism and Institutionalism are overall adjusted to diplomacy in the middle of states and non-state monetary substances in light of the fact that they presuppose the part of institutions in advancing collaboration between states. A Neomarxist-Gramscian approach's understanding of the material bases for state force offers an approach to separate between the force of states, and its rationale of transnational memorable alliances looking for the assent of the represented can clarify the inspiration to make encourage diplomacy and one of its fundamental destinations, collaboration and the consensual activity of force. From Social Constructivism we can draw upon thoughts of how states and much the same create and re-make their personalities through their public presentation of themselves and through arrangements, which thusly can move control between them.

From Postmodernism/Post-positivism, originations, for example, time-space clamping can clarify how the institutional association of representation has changed and how the rate of diplomatic communications has quickened, each of which support a few performers at the cost of others[40]. Neorealism's state-driven centre applies less well to the clarification of force in a diplomatic framework in which states themselves don't talk with one voice, and in the meantime, both venues for multilateral participation and performing artists with motivation and destinations different from those of any state. Notwithstanding being hard to place inside any single hypothetical custom, Strange's idea of

[40] Faith, Robert. "Rescuing Trade from Necessity: Henry Kissinger's Economic Diplomacy Toward the Soviet Union." Order No. 1498493, Indiana University of Pennsylvania, 2011. In PROQUESTMS ProQuest Dissertations & Theses Full Text, http://search.proquest.com/docview/894086273?accountid=120 85.

structural power as force to shape the parameters inside which others must settle on choices appears to be especially valuable in clarifying power in government-NSEE diplomatic associations (Strange, 1994, 1996). Utilizing Strange's four interlocking structures of information, generation, fund and security one can represent differences of force between states, the specific force concerned with worldwide back, and even the effect of the variability in aptitudes of diplomats on diverse sides of an arrangement. Case in point, Strange's methodology would anticipate that have a tendency to win in transactions with creating nations.

While the extension and perceivability of what I have termed the new public diplomacy is novel, the systems that it utilizes are definitely not. Influence, encircling, and agenda setting are the fundamental instruments of political impact. Nonetheless, concentrating on them has a tendency to change our understanding of how power works. The progressions in the political and correspondences setting of universal governmental issues change make their operation more unmistakable and open to more specialists. Force is not an enchantment projectile that can render the associations of global legislative issues instantly fathomable, however serves as short hand for what specialists do. The investigation displayed above recommends that we have been searching for force in the wrong places.

IR hypothesis has a tendency to begin from the assumption that military force is a definitive determinant of the results in IR. This military inclination brings about force being considered as far as meetings between decently characterized positions. The picture of force can be shown on the off chance that we think about the powers required to move a gigantic rock safely installed in a mountainside. Yet in the event that the stone is now moving down the mountain, the strengths required to push it in another bearing are all that much less. We may be not able to move the rock, yet in the event that it is as of now in movement, we may have the capacity to move it onto another course. Human culture (and especially the little segments of it that speak to political associations) is now (and constantly in movement), along these lines, a moderately minor driving force conveyed at the perfect place and time and can change conclusions.

To think regarding techniques is to see that the instruments of delicate force are not extraordinary yet the typical apparatuses of governmental issues. All that the new public diplomacy is doing is permitting more individuals to utilize them as a part of a more public way. The result of the time of blended media is that more individuals can do this changing the flow and the results of governmental issues, and that is no little thing. Anthony Giddens treats power and, by augmentation, org, as far as the ability to utilize the standards and assets that exist in any social setting to create impacts. What the new public diplomacy shows is the path in which mechanical and political change is changing the potential outcomes to act inside world legislative issues. Power needs to be dealt with as far as mobilization courses of action rather as far as structures or operators[41].

The progressions in the worldwide media environment influence the political methodologies embraced by both states and also non-state performers. Examination of these advancements recommends that power in the data age can't be seen singularly as far as assets or structures without thought of methodology issues, for example, assembling techniques and the capacity of operators to set plans and impact the confining of issues by means of the media. Such a viewpoint clarifies the capacity of asset poor performing artists to apply impact specifically circumstances and the limits of this impact.

EU International Relations and Diplomacy

The European Union is without a doubt a 'soft power', which uses as its main instrument the tool of diplomacy. Moreover, the EU is a soft power that tries to export its values and norms. One of the ways to do that is by use of the public diplomacy,

[41] Gottfried, Matthew Stuart. "The Origins and Consequences of Public Opinion in Coercive Terrorist Crises." Order No. 3621755, University of California, Los Angeles, 2014. In PROQUESTMS ProQuest Dissertations & Theses Full Text, http://search.proquest.com/docview/1545890466?accountid=12 085.

where the European Commission delegations (EC delegations) have a prominent place. It raise a question of what the role of the EC delegations in EU public diplomacy (EUPD) efforts is and to what extent these delegations can promote the value-based image of the EU in the world, as well as what can be achieved through that process of image creation[42].

EC delegations play a key role in the EUPD. As actors on the ground they are the first who, with their activities, can enforce the image of the EU in the third countries promoting its norms and values. Moreover, that external process can enhance the efforts of the EU identity building. The paper will focus on public diplomacy because, in the globalized world, public diplomacy plays an increasingly important role. The European public diplomacy will be a very useful tool for the EU to project itself and because, from most of the EU foreign policy initiatives, this seems the most consistent one and a unique tool in the modern diplomacy if not alternative diplomacy in the case of the EU. Moreover, the EUPD can pave the way in the future creation of EU identity in the framework of EU diplomacy.

---

[42] Gummer, S. C. "The Politics of Sympathy: German Turcophilism and the Ottoman Empire in the Age of the Mass Media 1871--1914." Order No. 3433144, Georgetown University, 2011. In PROQUESTMS ProQuest Dissertations & Theses Full Text, http://search.proquest.com/docview/835067334?accountid=120 85.

Public Diplomacy as Image Maker

The image of the EU in the world is very important, especially when the EU is "an unfinished political system" with very complicated structures and with increasing foreign policy objectives. This constant transformation of the EU (through its integration process, enlargements, new institutions etc.) results in the diffused image of the Union in the outside world, making its structures and policy objectives incomprehensible for the others, decreasing the influence of the EU. "How the country is perceived abroad has implications for that country's ability to attract tourism and investments. How a state is viewed by foreign publics can impact on its ability to engage with that country's government, and its ability to operate diplomatically or militarily". The tool which the EU uses to explain its policies is Public Diplomacy.

Public diplomacy is often referred as "a euphemism for propaganda". G.R. Berridge argues that "public diplomacy is the modern name for white propaganda directed chiefly at foreign publics". The importance of public diplomacy has increased over recent decades, especially since the end of the Cold War, when many non-governmental actors started to play greater role in the field of politics. In the multilateral and globalized world of today, the change and the adaptation of diplomacy to the environment was necessary, so that modern diplomacy is heavily based on its public diplomacy.

The EU has recognized public diplomacy as an important instrument in its soft power politics, whereas promotion of its values and norms is of key prominence. This alternative way of thinking and acting of the European Union have led to consideration of the Union as an alternative power. The EC delegations are "central to EU public diplomacy efforts". More than 130 EU delegations all over the world, "increase awareness of the EU; ensure broad understanding of EU policies, initiatives and messages and build relationships with state and local officials, community and business leaders, the media, students, and civil society". The EC delegations are unique structures in history, because, as M. Bruter argues, they have a role of embassies without a support of a state with its classical meaning whereas they had to reshape the classical meaning of the traditional diplomacy "by focusing on 'consumer-oriented' diplomatic services"[43].

All EC delegations are equipped with staff specialized in press and information activities. They are the extension of the EU policies on the ground where they are the primary sources of the EU in the contact with the third countries. S.B.Rasmussen argues, that the importance of the delegations in the framework of the EU public diplomacy is reflected in

[43] Klein, Adam Gordon. "A Quiet Road to War: Media Compliance and Suppressed Public Opinion in Iran." Order No. 3402791, Howard University, 2010. In PROQUESTMS ProQuest Dissertations & Theses Full Text, http://search.proquest.com/docview/305212388?accountid=120 85.

the important size of the budget designed for the delegations. Moreover, he underlines, that this amount is not distributed equally among different delegations, but reflects the priorities in EU external relations, such as the US for example. Just to give an example, in one of many issues of defocus , a magazine which promotes the EU, the topic was " The EU: a Community of Values", where it was explained that the EU is not only an economic or geographic community but also an "entity of values and standards, a unity of good in the world with moral depths" together with the photograph of Mr. Barroso with religious leaders.

Moreover, the EC/EU delegations try not only to present the core messages of the EU, but also, based on concrete cases, to highlight the EU success stories. At the same time the delegations are trying to influence foreign political discourses, promoting issues of central importance to the EU; for example climate change, where the EU is a leader, the problem is real and requires multilateral cooperation.

The EC delegations many times also cooperate along with the national embassies of the member states and organized some of the European level activities, in order to promote European history, culture and values. They also try to maintain the coherence between them to enhance the understanding of the EU as one entity. "The delegations used the 50th anniversary events to reinforce the EU's core messages".

De Gouveia argues that the delegations organize many public diplomacy activities without guidance or consultation with Brussels, where "quality and quantity vary according to the skills of delegations staff". Most of them include visits around the country, contact with local actors in schools and universities, publications, local media monitoring, journalist training programmes and other activities to promote "civil society dialog". Moreover, De Gouveia gives examples of EC delegations in Moscow and Washington, two strategic places for the EU. He underlines the range of their capabilities and conducted activities in the field of public diplomacy, where their connections with the host country became more familiar and allowed for reencounter of involved parts.

One of the problems of the EUPD, is that public diplomacy has to show the image of the EU, something that is closely related to a projection of an identity. The EC delegations "deprived of a unique , powerful head of state, strong administration, unified political positions to defend and promote, and a common diplomatic 'culture' (…) had to find some adaptive and original ways to formulate and carry out their activities"[44]. This is one of the reasons why the EUPD in the outside world managed by the EC

---

[44] Krzakowski, Caroline Zoe. "Aftermath: Foreign Relations and the Postwar British Novel." Order No. NR78789, McGill University (Canada), 2012. In PROQUESTMS ProQuest Dissertations & Theses Full Text, http://search.proquest.com/docview/1151101458?accountid=12085.

delegations had to force the development of 'some kind of' identity to represent. This development was based on the common history, culture, values and the common objectives of the European member states. The EUPD helped to increase the level of EU politico-cultural integration outside the EU, which could have as a result a spill-over to the inside and/or pave the way to the EU identity of the future EU diplomats. The role concept here is very important, where the 'logic of appropriateness' is a central element, so that the Union will start to behave according to how it has projected itself to the international society.

Last but not least, we have the basis to build on as Yan Xuetong from Tsinghua University in China underlines: "It seems to me that in European eyes, there is no common European identity. But in Chinese eyes it seems that you are all the same.(...) In our eyes you are all Europeans".

The Lisbon Treaty will further enhance EU public diplomacy, where the EC delegations will turn into the EU delegations and will have the central role in the creation of the image of the EU abroad, supported with the European External Action Service (EEAS). The EEAS will serve as EU diplomatic corps and will include all the diplomatic instruments along with the public diplomacy programs.

EU uses public diplomacy in order to increase the knowledge of its structure and moreover to promote its core values and norms in the world.

Public diplomacy is used as an important tool, because of its increased value in the framework of modern diplomacy in the globalized world. In the unique EU structure we can even argue that the Union has developed alternative diplomacy. The role of the EC/EU delegations is crucial in the effectiveness of this task, where they have the prominent role in implementation of the EUPD as the actors on the ground, dealing directly with the external actors.

Through different tasks the EC/EU delegations are conducting in the field of the public policy they above all project the image of the EU, and moreover we can argue that they project EU identity. The image that is created is perceived as one of the EU as coherent actor, and Union of values based on its historical and cultural developments. This creation of EU identity that is projected outside the EU, can be used as the basis for future EU diplomacy supported with the EEAS.

Public Diplomacy Overview and Development of a New Paradigm

Although the term "public diplomacy" was not coined until 1965, the practice of public diplomacy is as old as the United States. Broadly defined as the "influence of public attitudes on the formation and execution of foreign policies," public diplomacy is a key part of a nation-states survival (United States Information Agency Alumni Association 2008, "What is Public Diplomacy?"). The Founding Fathers of the U.S. were subject to the influence of public opinion and understood that they needed to appeal to the minds of decision-makers and publics abroad in order to rally support for an unprecedented war against Britain's Empire. Author J. Michael Waller points out that communication with international publics during the American Revolution was critical to building support from elements within the British Empire and among Britain's European rivals. Early forms of public diplomacy took shape as information operations employed during the American Revolution and served to mobilize a global coalition of supporters for American independence and democracy.

While early public diplomacy was primarily motivated by winning the American Revolution it continued to be recognized and reflected in the make-up of early diplomacy efforts. When Thomas Jefferson served as U.S. Secretary of State he recognized the importance of communication and appointed a messenger to serve as one of only six members of his staff. While history illustrates an early recognition of the importance of communication, the term "public diplomacy" reflects a relatively new field of practice and study. Public diplomacy has historically been an intuitive function for the U.S. Department of State which serves as America's voice and face abroad through overseas embassies, ambassadors and Foreign Service Nationals.

The end of the Cold War was accompanied by a downsizing of U.S. public diplomacy efforts that left the U.S. unprepared for the new challenges of the 21st century. The events of September 11th and the subsequent "War on Terror" highlighted the need for increased mutual understanding around the world and elevated the importance of public diplomacy. Joshua Fouts, former director of the University of Southern California Centre on Public Diplomacy, notes that successful public diplomacy can help to make a country not just more respected but more admired and liked. Since September 11th, scholars and practitioners have conducted over six comprehensive studies on public diplomacy and cite the need for an updated approach in the 21st century. The prevailing schools of thought in international relations, political science and communication have shed light into the necessity of public diplomacy. However, existing theories and historical research have not produced a working theory or model for categorizing and understanding various types of public diplomacy efforts[45].

Public diplomacy is multi-faceted and employs efforts that range from long-term goals of building mutual understanding around the world to short-term strategies such as countering immediate threats from violent extremism. In order to fully understand the role of public diplomacy in foreign affairs, we must understand the different types of activities under the umbrella of public diplomacy. The four existing communication and international relations-based theories and builds on relevant components to develop a new paradigm for understanding public diplomacy activities.

Relevant Theorists:

Public diplomacy activities are wedded to communication and international affairs. The initial intent of early public diplomacy activities was to communicate with foreign publics in an attempt to influence their opinions, beliefs and actions during times of war. This link to public diplomacy makes communication and international relations theories helpful to constructing an analytical framework for understanding the role of public diplomacy in foreign policy. Within international relations theory, critical theorist, Jurgen Habermas, of the Frankfort School,

---

[45] Lu, Yanqin. "Do Netizens Overlook "Official Frames" in China a Framing Analysis of Online News and Micro-Blogging Posts." Order No. 1538573, Indiana University, 2013. In PROQUESTMS ProQuest Dissertations & Theses Full Text, http://search.proquest.com/docview/1373382149?accountid=12085.

identifies two distinctly different types of actions in communication:

1) communication which is intended to increase mutual understanding; and
2) communication which is intended to persuade or co-opt.

Both of these forms of communication are used in foreign policy and according to Habermas are distinctly different due to the underlying motives and intentions which drive them. The intention behind communication is critical to Habermas because he contends that "communicative action," which focuses on non manipulative communication and language that builds mutual understanding, is preferable to persuasive communication because it facilitates higher levels of freedom by "binding norms through speech and debate. Within public diplomacy policy, the Fulbright-Hayes Act, which seeks to build mutual understanding between the U.S. and other countries, is an example of Habermas' concept of discourse communication. Habermas contends that discourse communication is important because building mutual understanding produces actions compatible with those understandings[46].

---

[46] Mackey, Timothy Ken. "Global Governance and Diplomacy Solutions for Counterfeit Medicines." Order No. 3567710, University of California, San Diego, 2013. In PROQUESTMS ProQuest Dissertations & Theses Full Text, http://search.proquest.com/docview/1417990538?accountid=12085.

The ability to influence not only attitudes about the U.S. but also action is critical to the success of U.S. public diplomacy. Habermas recognized the U.S. faces new challenges to establishing democracy on a global scale because it is difficult to communicate universal values that all cultures identify with. He notes that for cosmopolitan democracy to be successful it must "link people and cultures that do not have a common language, common symbols, or the shared history that have underpinned nation-states for the past two centuries" (Griffiths 2007, 48). As the geopolitical landscape changes in the 21st century, practitioners will increasingly find that

public diplomacy efforts need to provide these missing linkages. While public diplomacy policies can be viewed through the lens of communicative action because they employ language as a tool for influencing behaviour, further research is needed to directly apply communication theory to public diplomacy efforts.

Communication and international relations theories provide a foundation for understanding the different types of communication practitioners employ. However, scholars have noted that theories such as Habermas' "communicative action" are not enough for us to understand the various dimensions of interaction and communication styles in public diplomacy. For example, communications scholar Peter Dahlgren, argues that Habermas' theory of "communicative action," favours collaboration and "non-manipulative communication," over strategic and persuasive communication which Habermas calls strategic action or instrumental rationality. Habermas' theory focuses on this specific area of communication and leaves much room open for other theorists to build upon and identify categories of communication.

Within the field of international relations, several other theories apply to public diplomacy. International relations scholar, Joseph Nye, complements the foundation provided by Habermas by specifically linking theoretical concepts of power to public diplomacy. Nye contends public diplomacy is a key part of increasing a nations "soft power," which can be understood as the attractiveness of a country's "culture, political ideals, and policies". Public diplomacy efforts such as Voice of America, which broadcasts news and U.S. culture around the world, or international people to people exchanges such as the Fulbright program, often enhance "soft power," by highlighting the attractiveness of U.S. cultural, political and educational capital. Habermas' concept of communicative action overlaps with Nye's concept of three dimensions of public diplomacy in that they both identify key types of communication and differentiate between strategic communication and building mutual understanding. Unlike Habermas, Nye directly applies communication to public diplomacy and identifies three "dimensions" of public diplomacy: 1) "daily communication," the day to day articulation of foreign policy; 2) "strategic communication," development of a simple theme; and 3) "Development of lasting relationships," through efforts such as scholarship, exchanges, etc. Nye's identification of these different dimensions of communication in public diplomacy provides the foundation for developing a lens through which to view the way the U.S. communicates with the rest of the world[47].

At the core of both Nye and Habermas' differentiation of communication is a key debate on the function of public diplomacy: should public diplomacy efforts serve

1) a strategic policy function;
2) as a mouthpiece within the foreign affairs apparatus; or
3) as a tool to build mutual understanding.

Both Nye and Habermas shed light on this debate by distinguishing between communication that is intended to increase mutual understanding and that which is intended to persuade or coerce. By acknowledging that there are differences in the way the U.S. communicates with international publics these theories provide a basis for developing a new paradigm which places public diplomacy activities into three main categories. In addition to the foundation laid by Habermas and Nye, theories on

[47] Ramirez, Shawn Ling. "Accountability and International Conflict." Order No. 3600457, University of Rochester, 2013. In PROQUESTMS ProQuest Dissertations & Theses Full Text, http://search.proquest.com/docview/1465055637?accountid=12085.

public opinion and information as an element of power are helpful to understanding the different functions of public diplomacy. Theorists John Dewey and Walter Lippmann provide relevant insight into public diplomacy through their writings on public opinion, participatory democracy and mass media. For example, John Dewey's concept of discourse theory is linked to public diplomacy policies that emphasize engagement and the exchange of people and ideas.

Dewey's focus on the importance of communication and dialog in a participatory democracy sparked Habermas' belief in the effectiveness of non manipulative communication in expanding democracy. Dewey believed the linchpin of successful democracy rested in actively engaged citizens participating in the political process through communication and dialog. This concept of public and participatory democracy falls in line with public diplomacy efforts such as educational and cultural exchanges. Dewey, similar to Nye and Habermas, distinguishes between manipulative communication and communication which seeks to build dialogue and understanding. Within these types of communication, Dewey cites strategic communication, "communication that advances interest-based calculations," as less relevant to a participatory democracy. Dewey's communication preference has been cited by some scholars as being narrowly focused and less relevant to practical elements of communication that emphasize advocacy, persuasion, policies and strategic communication campaigns. Dewey, Habermas and Nye's emphasis on the intention behind communication lays a foundation for developing a new paradigm for public diplomacy[48].

All three theorists can be applied to public diplomacy because they draw a clear distinction between the motives, intentions and spirit of public communication. While the first three theorists suggest a nation's focus should be on building mutual understanding, Walter Lippmann, takes a pragmatic approach to communication and focuses on targeted communication in the form of propaganda and psychological warfare. Lippmann argues that propaganda cannot be divorced from politics because people's actions are influenced by their internal perception and imagery which is based not on direct and certain knowledge, but on pictures made by himself or given to him. The focus of Lippmann's communication theory is advocacy, persuasion and strategic campaigns which he believes are critical to shaping the mental filters that influence public opinion.

Lippmann's concept of communication is important because it provides insight into another

[48] Palkki, David Dean. "Deterring Saddam Hussein's Iraq: Domestic Audience Costs and Credibility Assessments in Theory and Practice." Order No. 3610480, University of California, Los Angeles, 2013. In PROQUESTMS ProQuest Dissertations & Theses Full Text, http://search.proquest.com/docview/1500437527?accountid=12085.

category of communication and highlights a different approach to public diplomacy. The concept of strategic communication, the combination of message and action, is widely used in public diplomacy efforts initiated by the U.S. Department of Defence (DOD) and the Central Intelligence Agency (CIA). An example of DOD's use of strategic communication is the creation of AFRICOM, which serves the objective of increasing global security through engaging in public diplomacy on the behalf of the U.S. within Africa. The creation of AFRICOM reflects Nye's concept of "smart power" which seeks to combine elements of hard and soft power to achieve foreign policy goals. Critics of Dewy and Habermas argue that Lippmann's concept of strategic communication is more practical than mutual understanding based communication because it accounts for the way "we make sense of a complex, confusing external world"[49]. As the global village increasingly bombards people and cultures with a plethora of messages, public diplomacy efforts must become more targeted, credible and aimed at commonalities if it is to generate both positive opinion and positive behaviours towards the U.S. While communication and international relations theories provide a basis for analyzing some elements

---

[49] Mutsaka, Chiedza Michelle. "Changing Foreign Public Perceptions through Culture Comparative Study of the Cultural Diplomacy of France and China in the Mekong Sub-Region." Order No. 1525312, Webster University, 2013. In PROQUESTMS ProQuest Dissertations & Theses Full Text, http://search.proquest.com/docview/1531128195?accountid=12 085.

of public diplomacy, there has not been a complete theory developed to help understand the underlying factors that influence public diplomacy policies. In order to gain additional insight into these factors, a new paradigm for public diplomacy is needed.

Towards a New Paradigm:

Recent works by scholars and practitioners have provided historical accounts of the mission, institution and practice of public diplomacy and identify the need for further research that explains underlying influences of public diplomacy. This section seeks to expand upon historical research, communication and international relations-based theory to create a new paradigm for categorizing public diplomacy efforts. The new paradigm seeks to help us understand public diplomacy policies by identifying three categories of policies:

1) Near-term;
2) Forward-looking; and
3) Long-term.

These categories are based on an analysis of efforts primarily put forth by key U.S. government agencies such as the U.S. Department of State. Near-term (NT) Efforts this category represents public diplomacy policies that are driven by pragmatic foreign policy goals and seek to promote the immediate priorities of U.S. foreign policy in a rapidly changing political environment. These public diplomacy policies seek to inform, promote and convince the world of the legitimacy of the U.S. foreign policy agenda and often serve as an immediate outlet for rapid response to international events. Near-term policy is reflective of Nye's definition of daily communications and is characterized by immediate communication that explains the domestic and foreign policy decisions of the U.S. Near-term policies, by definition, respond to shifts in the geopolitical landscape and are reactive as opposed to proactive policies. These policies reflect the priorities of an administration or political environment and are most effective when the message is seen as credible and the policy position is viewed as legitimate. The articulation of U.S. foreign policy is a critical element of public diplomacy because it sets the tone for U.S. interactions with the rest of the world. Near-term policies are inherently linked to foreign policy and are reliant on the standing and international perception of U.S. foreign policy.

When U.S. foreign policy is perceived as consistent with universal values the U.S. supports and as having genuine moral authority it serves as an effective tool of public diplomacy. However, when foreign policies are viewed as illegitimate, positive public opinion of the U.S. government declines and hurts U.S. political capital and by extension, U.S. soft power. Nye's example of near-term public diplomacy efforts is daily communications, which serves to explain "the context of domestic and foreign policy decisions"[50]. Nye argues that soft and hard power combined creates smart power, which cannot be achieved through short-term policies alone, but rather through long-term policies and strategic public diplomacy efforts.

Near-term public diplomacy policies employ Lippmann's concept of strategic communication because they are rooted in pragmatism and focus on public diplomacy efforts that are "goal oriented, driven by interest-based preferences and decisions and linked to power and the market". In addition, near-term policies typically employ strategic communication to meet pragmatic goals. For example, in 2007, the State Department's Undersecretary for Public Diplomacy, Karen Hughes, announced the first formal strategic plan for public diplomacy. The second strategic goal in the plan was to isolate and marginalize violent extremism. This goal reflects the priorities of the administration and the political landscape of the "War on Terror." These types of policies fall under the near-term category because they focus on specific priorities and goals of an administration.

Near-term policies are at the frontline of rapidly responding to international affairs and stir up

---

50 Marinova, Nadejda Kirilova. "House of Lebanon: How Host States use Diasporas---the George W. Bush Administration and the Lebanese-American Lobby." Order No. 3466054, University of Southern California, 2011. In PROQUESTMS ProQuest Dissertations & Theses Full Text, http://search.proquest.com/docview/884339035?accountid=120 85.

a fundamental debate: should public diplomacy serve to promote/address near term policy goals or long-term objectives of building relationships? Should public diplomacy represent the broader interests of a country or the imperatives of an incumbent president? The following chapters will explore the historical influences on public diplomacy and shed light on the role of public diplomacy in foreign policy[51]. Forward-looking Efforts are categorized as policies driven by U.S. political values and attempt to align fundamental values and beliefs with foreign policy priorities. Forward-looking public diplomacy policies reflect elements of the concept of strategic communication and are longer in duration than near-term policies. These policies typically send a message of the overall purpose of public diplomacy in a nation-state's foreign affairs. These policies are characterized, in part, by Joseph Nye's concept of strategic communication in that these public diplomacy efforts develop a set of simple themes much as political or advertising campaigns do.

Nye notes that strategic communication functions like a campaign because it reinforces a central set of themes and occurs over the course of a year to brand central themes, or to advance a particular government policy. An example of forward

[51] Labinski, Nicholas. "Evolution of a President: John F. Kennedy and Berlin." Order No. 1496774, Marquette University, 2011. In PROQUESTMS ProQuest Dissertations & Theses Full Text, http://search.proquest.com/docview/890109254?accountid=120 85.

looking policy is the U.S. Department of State's Under Secretary for Public Diplomacy and Public Affairs, Jim Glassman's focus on a targeted campaign of the "War of Ideas." This initiative, launched in June of 2008, is specific and aims to focus on counterterrorism. Glassman notes that:

. . .unlike traditional functions of public diplomacy like education and cultural exchanges, the aim of the war of ideas is not to persuade foreign populations to adopt more favourable views of the United States and its policies. Instead, the war of ideas tries to ensure that negative sentiments and day-to-day grievances toward the U.S. and its allies do not manifest themselves in the form of violent extremism.

This public diplomacy policy reflects forward-looking policy because the initiative is a clear, targeted message, that is carried out over the course of Undersecretary Glassman's political appointment. As the U.S. seeks to counter terrorism through public diplomacy, Habermas' concept of communicative action is particularly relevant for forward-looking and mutual understanding-based policies because it identifies the challenge of spreading democracy across the globe and links its success to an ability to increase dialogue and mutual understanding based policies. Forward-looking policies differ from near-term policies in that they operate for a specified amount of time and are pre-meditated. A majority of U.S. public diplomacy efforts focus on the rhetoric and the delivery of a policy message and hence fall under the category of forward-looking efforts.

Long-term Efforts are categorized as public diplomacy that focuses on developing mutual understanding by harnessing U.S. cultural resources to increase the nation's attractiveness to others. These policies are characterized by action in the form of people to people exchanges of art, education, science and culture. An example of long-term policy includes educational and cultural exchange programs such as the Fulbright Scholarship, the International Visitor Leadership program and the Jazz Ambassadors program. Nye gives examples of long-term policies as the "development of lasting relationships with key individuals, over many years through scholarships, exchanges, training, seminars, conferences and access to media channels". Actions or in Habermas' case "communicative action" is critical to public diplomacy policies because it distinguishes between communication that is intended to build mutual understanding from that which is intended to coerce or co-opt. These policies employ the concept of discourse communication because they incorporate the "social collective and their cultures to share meaning and understanding, by listening and building a sphere where "diverse voices can be heard.

Scholars argue long-term policies such as exchanges are critical to public diplomacy because they build mutual understanding which is believed to shape behaviour. Long-term policies that build mutual understanding and dialogue are also linked to achieving pragmatic goals. Author Bruce Gregory notes that exchanges, a key long-term policy, achieve a variety of second order goals such as: . . .reduction of tensions and negative attitudes toward the U.S., eliminate the fertile ground that terrorist recruiters exploit, influence the next generation of leaders, communicate freedom and democracy, justice and opportunity, diversity and tolerance, combat anti-Americanism and misperceptions that threaten U.S. security.

Long-term policies serve both pragmatic and altruistic goals in that they function to build mutual understanding and promote support for democratic values. In November 2007, U.S. Secretary of Defence, Robert Gates noted the need for the U.S. to increase its soft power. He acknowledged that the U.S.: Must focus our energies beyond the guns and steel of the military, beyond just our brave soldiers, sailors, Marines, and airmen. We must also focus our energies on the other elements of national power that will be so crucial in the coming years. Gates focus on soft power is telling of the role that public diplomacy plays in foreign affairs. Long-term policies reinforce that public diplomacy is not merely a mouthpiece for foreign policy but rather a channel for increasing dialogue and understanding. Despite the pragmatic purposes of long-term policies such as educational and cultural exchanges, critics of long-term mutual understanding policies argue that public diplomacy should focus more on promoting ideals over developing dialog. These three categories of public diplomacy efforts provide a critical lens for identifying underlying values, assumptions and trends[52].

By categorizing the major types of activities employed by public diplomacy, it becomes evident that it is a multi-faceted field with competing priorities, timeframes and goals. Understanding the underlying values and assumptions that drive public diplomacy will help to provide a more thorough lens to analyze public diplomacy in the 21st century.

---

[52] Khamidov, Alisher. "The Base of Contention: Kyrgyzstan, Russia and the U.S. in Central Asia (2001--2010)." Order No. 3483028, The Johns Hopkins University, 2011. In PROQUESTMS ProQuest Dissertations & Theses Full Text, http://search.proquest.com/docview/902627242?accountid=120 85.

Applying the Paradigm to Four Themes in Public Diplomacy:

This thesis proposes that most U.S. public diplomacy efforts in the 21st century have been focused on near-term efforts that are driven by four underlying themes in public diplomacy:

1) ideology and foreign policy;
2) organizational politics;
3) competitive pressures from rivalry; (and)
4) leadership personalities and positions of influence.

These underlying themes have shaped the ideology, style, doctrines, perceptions, budgets, time horizons and organizational structures of U.S. public diplomacy. Because public diplomacy is carried out for interest and value based reasons, we must identify the themes that shape the role of public diplomacy in order to understand its capacity and limitations. The history, mission and practice of U.S. public diplomacy efforts serve as a basis for identifying the four major themes that are believed to influence public diplomacy policies. The new paradigm for public diplomacy provides an analytical framework that helps to categorize public diplomacy activities. The paradigm will be used to identify the extent to which the four themes influence public diplomacy policies that are:

1) near-term;

2) forward-looking; or
3) long-term.

By highlighting three categorizations, the new paradigm allows public diplomacy policies to be identified as aligned with one of the three categories. All of these categories employ advocacy techniques which Nicholas Crull in Public Diplomacy: Taxonomies and Histories describes as "an actor's attempt to manage the international environment by undertaking international communication activities to actively promote a particular policy, an idea or an actor's general interests in the minds of a foreign public. The new paradigm provides a distinction that will aid in identifying underlying values, trends and commonalities   across   the   four   themes. Understanding the core values and categories associated with public diplomacy policies will help forecast future public diplomacy efforts and provide insight into the areas that need to be adapted for the 21st century.

International Affairs and Diplomacy

The art and practice of conducting negotiations among the representatives of states or groups is commonly known as diplomacy. Normally it is referred to an international diplomacy that is the conduct of international relations with the intercession of professional diplomats. The issues that are mostly resolved by the process of diplomacy are related to trade, economics, human rights, environment, war and peace-making. The negotiation process is used by the diplomats on international treaties before the endorsement by national politicians. Diplomacy is an employment of tactics for gaining strategic advantage or to find out the mutual solutions that can be used for solving any issue like poverty, hunger, human rights protection etc. All the issues are resolved in a polite and non-confrontational manner among all the diplomats and national or international politicians[53]. International affairs and diplomacy are closely related to gathering or espionage of intelligence. Some of the diplomats are openly known as spies and embassies provide basis for them to plan out all the activities that can be beneficial for the society.

United Nations is an organisation that looks after the issues related to international affairs and diplomacy. United Nations provides institutions, mechanisms and standards that can assist the diplomats in resolving and identifying the solutions to the issues that are raised within the society. The role of media is of great importance in international affairs and diplomacy as it helps in keeping the people aware of the initiatives and activities that take place around the world. Mass media pays more attention towards the human rights issues and questions related to it and the focus is mainly on

[53] Jalali, Javad. "The Impact of Sanctions upon Civil Aviation Safety." Order No. MR83973, McGill University (Canada), 2011. In PROQUESTMS ProQuest Dissertations & Theses Full Text, http://search.proquest.com/docview/1033333572?accountid=12 085.

foreign policy and international relations. The human rights activists groups and NGO's can also play an effective role in managing the diplomacy and international relations or affairs with their own established platform. The issues related to poverty in the country can be effectively managed with the help of diplomacy and international affairs management. The meetings that are held among all the members of the United Nations Members are based on identifying solutions and raising the issues that are faced by the citizens of any particular state or country.

The diplomats need to prepare themselves about the issues that they are going to raise in the international meetings and conferences that are held under the umbrella of United Nations, so that they can maintain their stance effectively and keep themselves aligned to the societal, economic, human rights purposes. Human rights are the most raised issues on which extensive discussions are conducted. The main aim of raising these issues in the international meetings and conferences is to make the world aware of the situations for which the countries are going through. Medical facilities, poverty, education, security, health and sanitation etc are all the basic necessities of humans that needs to be fulfilled by the government but if the government is unable to fulfil all the needs of the public then they should raise their voice in the international meetings arranged by various institutions of the United Nations such as UNESCO, WHO etc. The human rights are still not given sufficient attention therefore still there are many issues found in entire world.

International affairs and diplomacy revolves around social, cultural, political and economic aspects of the countries or states. In the context of globalization and the end of the Cold War, one would have expected a revival of human rights as a genuine global venture capable of engaging and mobilizing mass constituencies[54]. Effective legal systems can be beneficial in handling the issues related to human rights. The formation of good governing bodies within the state or at country level can help in resolving the issues related to violations of human rights and will support the humanity. International affairs and diplomacy can help the developing and under developed countries in accomplishing their motives like fight against hunger, poverty, water dispute etc. in an effective way. United Nations Security Council is an institution that is working for providing security to all the states which are its members. It is striving to provide peaceful environment to all the countries of the world and encourages having good relations among all the countries. The projects related to international human rights are established to look after and fight for the rights of humans and to make their lives free from all the sufferings.

---

[54] Harmes, David T. "International Radio Broadcasting and Post-Conflict State-Building: The Case of Canada's Rana FM." Order No. NR93370, Ryerson University (Canada), 2012. In PROQUESTMS ProQuest Dissertations & Theses Full Text, http://search.proquest.com/docview/1350628046?accountid=12085.

The European Court of Human Rights along with the adjoin European Convention on Human Rights has helped Europe in forming effective regional system that is keeping good check over the issues related to human rights. The supervisory commissions, institutes and national human rights groups are also playing an effective role in most of the developing and developed countries for monitoring the issues related to human rights protection.

Furthermore, the national legislators and predominantly the national judiciaries often found manifesting an attitude of an activist when it comes to an implementation of human rights. In the struggle of public justice, the international human rights are not only supporting the humans in providing legal resources based on the state laws but it also anchors the political means in the public legitimacy. The international affairs keep the record of all the inter-related aspects that can be used as a reference in the international meetings but also provides them competitive edge in claiming their equitable portion. To "protect human rights," means protecting the interests of humans whose rights are not fulfilled. All these activities are handled with the reference and support of state law.

Hence, the entire picture offers a comprehensive perspective related to the commitment of the civilisation with utmost importance. In the nonexistence of reliable global mechanisms that can help in enforcement of the human rights, international human rights laws and principles need to be well connected, first and foremost, to national mechanisms and institutions with power to put into effect these standards. Undeniably, from an international legal perspective, state sovereignty may be well defended with the use of international affairs and diplomacy.

Influence of public relations on news content

In many studies in the area of media sociology, scholars have identified a number of factors that influence news content. Specifically, five categories of factors have been identified as influencing news content. According to scope of influence, these factors include (1) individual attributes (e.g., media professionals' education and gender); (2) media routines (e.g., gate keeping, beat system, and pack journalism); (3) organizational characteristics (e.g., political endorsements, editorial positions, and corporate policies); (4) extra-media variables (e.g., advertisers' and news sources' interventions); and (5) ideological influences (e.g., standard social values). According to Shoemaker and Reese (1991), in addition to competing media organizations, advertisers, audiences, and government controls, the public relations activities of a variety of news sources, such as interests groups and corporate organizations, can be considered extra-media organizational factors can significantly influence news content. Manheim (1987) also argued that external factors, including the strategic public relations efforts of news sources, may affect decisions about whether a topic is included or discarded in the news media agenda.

Many organizations consider their own appearance in the news media as a cost-effective way of reaching their publics. Press releases from different sources also assist journalists in identifying news items and fill news holes under tight deadlines. Indeed, Shoemaker (1991) explains that public relations activities affect news content directly by providing story ideas to the media that support an organization's position or indirectly by using the media to project organization-related issues onto the public agenda. Public relations practitioners also create pseudo-events, such as demonstrations and protests, to gain media attention and, subsequently, public attention, and these events serve move news content toward the direction intended by the source organizations. Turow (1989) pointed out that "public relations are a driving force behind what gets on television and into print" (p. 26). He notes that many news stories originate from press releases, indicating the "overwhelming importance of PR materials for the contemporary press" (p. 206). In the process, public relations practitioners "insinuate their ideas into hard news stories with the aim of attracting lawmakers' attention" (p. 208) and try to disguise their own political agenda from both the media and the public. In spite of its significant influence on the flow of news, however, the field of public relations has received limited attention from scholars. This neglect becomes more problematic considering the potential impact of public relations on international news content.

The empirical evidence that demonstrates public relations' effect on news content is sometimes contradictory. For example, Albritton and Manheim (1983) found that a public relations campaign improved Rhodesia's image in the U.S. press.

Stocking (1985), on the other hand, suggested limited effects of PR activities by saying that PR activities often do not go beyond news value. An issue's news value, Stocking suggests, is a more powerful predictor that an issue will appear in the news media agenda.

According to Manheim and Albritton (1984), professional and systematic public relations efforts in the U.S. on behalf of foreign governments noticeably increased in the 1970s, as suggested by the Foreign Agent Registration Records (FARA) of the Department of Justice. Since then, fostering a country's positive and favourable image in the U.S. news media has been an important goal that international clients try to achieve by contracting with American PR firms. Testing the effect of public relations intervention on the visibility and valence of U.S. news coverage about a foreign country, Manheim and Albritton (1984) found that national image, as portrayed in the news media, improved after the signing of contracts with PR firms in the U.S. This finding suggests that public relations can change how countries are portrayed in the news media of a target country.

However, recent empirical studies have shown a somewhat limited effect of international public relations activities on the news content of the foreign news media. Yoon (2005) organized previous studies that investigate the impact of PR on news content into two major categories: (1) acceptance or rejection of sources' information subsidies and the utilization of these information subsidies; and (2) journalists' perceptions of PR and PR persons and how these perceptions affect journalistic products. An organization can build legitimacy as a news source and can attract media attention by steadily providing journalists with information subsidies. According to Yoon (2005), "PR could be a key strategic choice to pursue, either to consolidate superior media access or to make frequent interventions as sources contend for media space" (p. 763). She found that although public relations efforts do not directly correlate with media access, media access can be increased by enhancing journalists' perceptions of the sources' legitimacy, which is significantly correlated with the quantity and quality of public relations efforts. The sources perceived as legitimate by journalists are likely to be covered more favourably and positively in the long term.

According to Lee (2004), the more public relations contracts foreign countries sign with PR agencies in the U.S., the more coverage those countries receive in the U.S. newspapers. He also found that the number of public relations contracts in the U.S. was positively correlated with a country's prominence in national newspapers and in network television news coverage. After controlling for environmental and relational factors, strategic public relations emerged as a significant factor explaining the variance in the prominence that countries enjoyed in U.S. newspaper coverage. He concluded that public relations may be associated with prominence in terms of length of stories published and where they are located in a newspaper edition, whereas the quantity of coverage is influenced by newsworthiness.

News media influence on public perception

Using structural theory, Galtung and Ruge (1965) explain that the economic, social, political, and geographic attributes of a country can affect how often and how favourably that country is described in another country's news media. In their theory, which emphasizes the critical role of the news media as image-projectors, they suggested a linear process of image formation through news coverage. In this model, the public's perception of a country is created through a series of steps although each step may introduce image distortions. Galtung and Ruge (1965) indicated that national image is shaped not only by the news media but also by a variety of information channels, such as personal contacts. The news media, however, remain "first-rate competitors for the number-one position as international image-former" because of their "regularity, ubiquity, and perseverance" (p. 64). Additionally, according to the media dependency theory, individuals generally rely on the media for the best available information to understand issues and to form their perceptions about them, especially when the issues are beyond their personal experience.

Manheim and Albritton (1984) also argue that the news media are often the major sources of the most up-to-date information regarding international affairs. However, the news media have a limited capacity in terms of covering all parts of the world. Thus, countries receive varying levels of coverage in the U.S. news media. Political, geographical, economic, and cultural considerations force the news media to assign different "weights" in their coverage of other countries[55]. This imbalance in the coverage of foreign countries in international news reporting may influence the public's perception of the salience of each country to their own countries and to their political lives and, consequently, public opinion toward them. The news media not only report foreign policy but also help shape foreign policy by galvanizing public opinion through their coverage.

Previous studies have examined the relationship between international news coverage and public opinion about foreign countries. For example, Semetko, Brzinski, Weaver, and Willnat (1992) analyzed U.S. network news and wire service coverage of nine countries (West Germany, East Germany, the Soviet Union, Hungary, Poland, Great Britain, France, Japan, and Israel), and compared it with public opinion about these nine countries gathered from the U.S. national public opinion surveys. The findings showed that the visibility of foreign countries in TV news significantly influenced public opinion about these countries. McNelly and

[55] Gary, David J. "Rufus King and the History of Reading: The use of Print in the Early American Republic." Order No. 3553074, City University of New York, 2013. In PROQUESTMS ProQuest Dissertations & Theses Full Text, http://search.proquest.com/docview/1314577167?accountid=12085.

Izcaray (1986) also concluded that mass media exposure was related to positive images of foreign countries in a given nation. Nisbet et al. (2004) found that Muslim audiences who choose Western networks as primary news channels have less negative perceptions of the U.S. than those who prefer the pan-Arab regional networks. Viewing the pan-Arab networks serves to "amplify" anti-American attitudes, but watching Western networks functions to "buffer or attenuate" this effect. This finding supports the idea that the selective use of media channels and biased contents has a bearing on public opinion toward a country. Many media effects studies have shown the influence of news coverage on public perceptions. The agenda-setting theory, which proposes the transfer of issue salience from the media agenda to the public agenda, is one of the traditional media effects theories often applied in studies of this kind.

CHAPTER 3: RESEARCH METHODOLOGY

Method

This study employs multiple methods of data gathering. First, secondary data were gathered and analyzed to determine international PR efforts of foreign countries from the semi-annual report generated through the Foreign Agency Registration Act (FARA). The results of the Chicago Council on Foreign Relations (CCFR) survey were also analyzed to examine U.S. public perceptions of select countries. Second, content analysis was conducted to reveal the nature of U.S. news coverage of foreign countries. Using these methods, this study examines the international public relations efforts conducted by foreign countries in the U.S., the U.S. news coverage of those countries, and U.S. citizens' perceptions of those countries.

Operationalization and measurement of international public relations

International public relations involve intentional activities governments undertake to influence foreign media and publics. According to Lee (2004), these activities include contracts with public relations agencies in a target country, the dissemination of press releases disseminations, and the management of a public information ministry or embassy. The funds dedicated to international PR and administrative expertise in public diplomacy are also potential factors that have a bearing on a country's ability to influence the foreign media and publics. Among these, according to Gilboa (2000), contracting public relations agencies in a target country is the most effective method that "strengthens the legitimacy and authenticity" of public relations efforts.

In this study, international public relations efforts were operationalized using two indicators: (1) the number of contracts foreign governments have signed with PR agencies in the U.S., and (2) the dollar amount of these contracts. These data were gathered from the semi-annual FARA reports. FARA was enacted by the U.S. Congress in 1938 because of significant concerns about the involvement of American PR agencies in German propaganda. Since then, PR agencies have been required to publicly report contracts involving international clients to the Department of Justice. Thus the FARA dataset has been the best available source of information regarding the diverse types of international public relations activities conducted in the U.S.

The data for this study came from the first semi-annual FARA report of 2002. Aside from the number of contracts and the contract prices used in this analysis, the report also includes other PR-related contract information from over 150 countries, sorted in alphabetical order (e.g., the PR agency involved and its contact information, the description of the contracted services, and the terms of the contract). The FARA report includes all PR contracts with all types of international clients such as individuals, political parties, and corporate organizations. However, only contracts by foreign central governments including foreign affair ministries and embassies were selected and counted to test main hypotheses in this study.

Operationalization and measurement of public perceptions (public diplomacy) of foreign countries

Public perception or public diplomacy of foreign countries was considered as having two dimensions, cognitive and affective evaluations, following Ghanem's (1997) and Wanta et al.'s (2004) conceptualizations. In this study, cognitive evaluation was defined as how significantly the American people perceive a country in relation to the U.S., while the affective evaluation was defined as how Americans feel about a given country. To measure these two aspects of public perceptions, the results of a U.S. national survey, conducted by the CCFR in June 2002, were collected. The CCFR is a non profit organization, and its quadrennial public opinion survey is regarded as the most comprehensive project exploring American attitudes toward a broad range of international relations issues, including U.S. foreign policy. The CCFR began its Worldviews Project in 1974, and the 2002 survey data is the most recent output available online (www.worldviews.org or www.ccfr.org). In the 2002 survey, with the collaboration of Harris Interactive, a randomly sampled set of 3,262 U.S. citizens were interviewed via telephone (n=2, 862) or in person (n=400) from June 1 to June 30, 2002.

Among a number of questions asked in the survey, two questions were utilized as a measure of U.S. public perception of foreign countries: perceived U.S. vital interest in foreign countries, and the public feelings toward these countries. The former was measured by the percentage of respondents who think the U.S. has a vital interest in a foreign country. The more people agreed that the country is of vital interest to the U.S., the higher the score a country received in this area. Public feelings involved emotional evaluations elicited when people were asked to rate each country on a scale from 0 to 100. Assuming the midpoint, 50, is neutral, numbers over 50 mean a positive feeling and numbers less than 50 indicate a negative feeling. The more positively and favourably individuals considered the country, the higher the score given to that country.

The FARA report and the CCFR's public opinion survey had 24 countries in common. These 24 countries constituted the complete list of countries (N=24) that targeted the U.S. with public relations efforts that were analyzed in this study.

Content analysis of news coverage

A content analysis of news coverage was conducted to examine how prominently the 24 countries were portrayed in the U.S. news media and valence of that coverage. Thus, news coverage of the 24 foreign countries in the U.S. press was analyzed for prominence and valence.

Sampling process

Two newspapers, the New York Times and the Washington Post, were selected for analysis. These newspapers are widely considered to have the strongest international news coverage and are most influential in reaching the opinions of U.S. leaders and the general public. These newspapers are also known to affect the content of other news media channels in the U.S. and overseas.

The full text of stories about the 24 countries published from January 1, 2002 to June 30, 2002, was retrieved from the Lexis-Nexis database. The period of analysis was identified by considering the time it takes to transfer an issue from the media agenda to the public agenda. Among a total of 4,302 articles retrieved from Lexis-Nexis, one-third were selected for analysis through a systematic sampling method. First, news articles were retrieved country by country by using the name of a given country as a search keyword in news headline. Then, every third articles were selected in each list of articles with having the first one in the list as a starting point.

Sampled articles were excluded for coding if the articles mentioned a country only in a peripheral way. Any news item in the Information Bank Abstracts, which is an abstract type of news article provided by the Wall Street Journal and published in the New York Times, was included for a analysis (i.e., the total number of articles), but was excluded in further coding for prominence and valence because they are too short (about 30 words in one or two sentences) to provide any sense of valence. If two or more countries were discussed in an article, the article was coded as pertaining only to the country of the primary actor. The actions of a country's citizens (e.g., crime, murder, fraud) in their own country and in the U.S. were included for analysis because the behaviours of citizens may affect public perceptions. Thus, if more than 20 percent of the samples for each country were excluded for these reasons, the same number of articles was substituted in the same sampling frame through a repeated systematic sampling method.

Prominence

Prominence, in this study, was measured by evaluating four indicators: (1) the number of news articles, (2) the length of coverage, (3) the position of stories within the coverage, and (4) the presence of supplementary graphic devices in the coverage. First, the total number of articles for each country was counted. The total number of articles has been used as a reliable indicator of intensity of coverage in many previous studies (e.g., Shoemaker, Damielian, & Brendlinger, 1991; Wanta et al., 2004; Manheim and Albritton, 1984). In addition, the length of the article was coded in terms of number of words, and the position of the articles within a newspaper edition was coded as a categorical variable: 3 = front page, 2 = section front page, 1 = other pages.

These two variables were added, following Shoemaker et al. (1991) and Lee (2004), because people are influenced not only by the sheer volume of stories but also by irregular and accidental exposure to coverage. Lastly, the use of supplementary graphic devices was coded: 1 = one or more graphic devices, 0 = no graphic device. Supplementary graphic devices include any visuals that accompany news articles, such as pictures, graphs, diagrams, tables, and cartoons or other illustrations. The presence of these graphic devices was determined by the caption information provided by Lexis-Nexis. Scholars note that visual cues in news stories, both in newspaper and television, have a significant effect on audiences' cognitive processes and response because they function as "capturing and sustaining attention, improving memory, and increasing arousal" (p. 317). For instance, Wanta (1988) points out that the size of photographs that accompany news stories influences readers' perception of the importance of that story.

A country enjoys high prominence in the news coverage when it is often covered by a target country's news media in longer and more in-depth stories, when the articles are presented in more visible space (such as the front page and the section top page), and when supplementary graphic devices are provided.

Valence

Valence is defined as the general orientation of news coverage and was assessed as (1) positive, (2) negative, or (3) neutral. Positive articles are those that discuss "progress, growth, prosperity, resources, strength, stability, and trustworthiness on the part of a given country." Negative stories discuss "unreliability, untrustworthiness, weakness, instability, retreat, and inefficiency on the part of a given country" (Lee, 2004, pp. 42–43). Wanta et al. (2004) saw a topic's conformity with U.S. interests and values as a global standard with which individuals judge whether the news is either positive or negative. In this study, if the primary foreign country described in the story threatened the interests of the U.S. or if its activity was inconsistent with U.S. values, the article was coded as negative. If the activity of a foreign country was seen as supporting U.S. interests or values, it was coded as positive.

Two coders were trained to follow the coding guidelines based on Lee's (2004) and Wanta et al.'s (2004) studies to decide whether the valence of an article is positive or negative. Table 1 shows common examples of positive or negative valence found during the content analysis.

Table 1. Examples of positive and negative valence

Examples of positive news	Examples of negative news
· **Growth of a country-origin companies**	· Loss of a country-origin companies (e.g., bankruptcy, decrease in sales, etc.)
· **Positive cooperation with the US**	· Lack of religious rights/freedoms.
	· Dangerous and unsafe environment (e.g., bombings, terrorist threats, arms threats).
	· Conflict between countries and in-country (e.g., labour dispute, political tensions, etc.)
	· Turmoil and violence.
	· Devaluation of currency.
	· Natural disaster (e.g., earthquake).
	· Human disaster (e.g., airplane crash.

A neutral valence is defined as one in which neither positive nor negative aspects of a country are discussed or as one demonstrating both positive and negative aspects of a given country in a balanced way. Thus, news articles about the outbreak of natural or human disasters were coded as negative, but those dealing with government and public efforts of restoration after the disasters were coded as neutral.

This study also considered valence proportion, which is defined as the ratio of the number of positive articles to the number of negative articles. Valence proportion recognizes that people are influenced by the different tones of the news items they encounter; the impact of positive representations of a country in the news may be balanced by that of negative representations. Therefore, the more positive coverage a country received compared to the negative coverage, the higher the score it attained in terms of valence proportion. Inter-coder reliability. To test for inter-coder reliability, 10 percent of the articles were systematically chosen and coded. The result of the Holsti formula for inter-coder reliability shows acceptable scores for the following coded variables: Country (1.00); Source (1.00); Date (1.00); Length (1.00); Position (1.00); Graphics (1.00); Valence (0.89).

Theoretical model

The proposed model of relationships among the variables is illustrated in Figure 4. In the figure, variables in rectangles denote observed variables, whereas the ones in ovals denote unobserved latent variables.

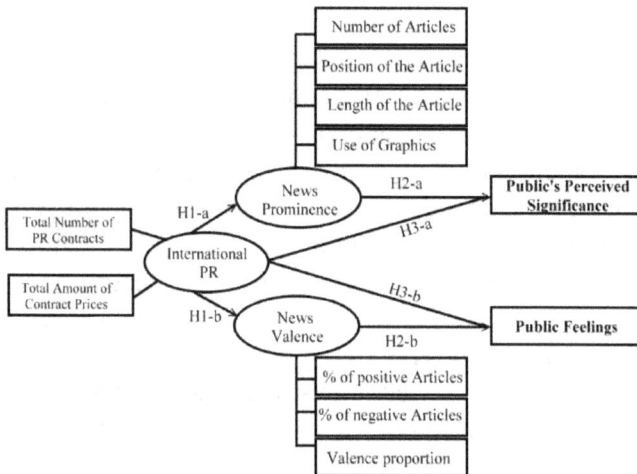

Figure 4. Theoretical model of the variables' relationships

CHAPTER 4: FINDINGS

To test the hypotheses and the degree of model fitness, the SPSS software programs were used.

Descriptive statistics
International PR

From the first semi-annual FARA report of 2002, the number of PR contracts and total dollar amount of the contracts by foreign central government including ministries and embassies, were counted and added. Table 1 shows how many PR contracts each country had in the U.S. and how much money was involved in these contracts. According to the FARA dataset, Japan, Mexico, Saudi Arabia, and Great Britain are the four countries that have the highest number of contracts and the highest total dollar amount of contracts with PR firms in the U.S. On the other hand, no government-based PR contracts were reported for Brazil and Russia. Brazil, Iran, Iraq, Nigeria, Pakistan, and Russia have few contracts, and thus little money was reported for these small numbers of contracts.

Public perceptions of foreign countries

The 2002 Worldviews report from the CCFR grouped countries that the U.S. public perceived to be of vital interest to the U.S.: (1) countries for which over 70% of respondents agreed the U.S. as having vital interest (Japan, Saudi Arabia, China,

Russia, Israel, Great Britain, Canada, Pakistan, Iraq, Iran, Afghanistan, and Mexico); (2) countries for which 51 to 70% of the respondents agreed (South Korea, Germany, Taiwan, India, Colombia, Egypt, France, and Turkey); and (3) countries for which under 50% of the respondents agreed (South Africa, Argentina, Brazil, and Nigeria).

Table 1. Number of PR contracts and the dollar amount (from the 2002 FARA report)		
Country	Number of PR contracts by foreign central government	Dollar amount of PR contracts by foreign central government ($)
Afghanistan	2	30000
Argentina	4	125000
Brazil	0	0
Canada	2	752426
China	4	468254
Colombia	2	385603
Egypt	4	600688
France	15	717660
Germany	1	91980
Great Britain	7	6721831
India	4	1873737
Iran	5	5793
Iraq	1	0
Israel	4	444772
Japan	17	4886009
Mexico	11	3008663
Nigeria	3	300000
Pakistan	2	300408
Russia	0	0
Saudi Arabia	9	6818764
South Africa	2	2839060
South Korea	6	1457811
Taiwan	2	91700
Turkey	5	1077018

Statistics regarding the public's perceived significance of these countries is provided in Table 2.

Table 2. Public perceptions of foreign countries (from the 2002 CCFR survey)		
Country	Public's perceived significance	Public feelings
Afghanistan	73	29
Argentina	39	47
Brazil	36	55
Canada	76	77
China	83	48
Colombia	62	36
Egypt	53	45
France	53	55
Germany	68	61
Great Britain	78	76
India	65	46
Iran	75	28
Iraq	76	23
Israel	79	55
Japan	83	60
Mexico	72	60
Nigeria	31	42
Pakistan	76	31
Russia	81	55
Saudi Arabia	83	33
South Africa	49	50
South Korea	69	46
Taiwan	65	50
Turkey	52	45

* Public's perceived significance was measured by the percentage of respondents who agreed that the country is of vital interest to the U.S.

* Public feelings was measured on a scale from 0 to 100; with the midpoint, 50, as neutral, over 50 represents a positive feeling while under 50 represents a negative feeling.

The Worldviews report also measures how the U.S. public feels about these countries by asking respondents to rate them on a scale from 0 to 100. Considering the midpoint, 50, as representing a neutral feeling, a score of over 50 indicates a positive and favourable feeling and a score under 50 indicates a negative feeling. According to the report, Canada (77) and Great Britain (76) are at the top of the scale, followed by Germany (61), Japan (60), and Mexico (60). Russia, Israel, Brazil, France, Taiwan, South Africa, China, Argentina, India, South Korea, Turkey, Egypt, and Nigeria are in the mid-range, between the 40s and 50s on the scale. At the same time, U.S. citizens feel negatively about the following countries: Iraq (23), Iran (28), Afghanistan (29), Pakistan (31), Saudi Arabia (33), and Colombia (36). Content analysis of news coverage. Among the 4,302 articles retrieved, 1,277 articles (approximately 30%) were sampled. The number of articles published in the New York Times articles in the sample is twice as large as the number of Washington Post articles. A total of 865 (67.7%) articles were from the New York Times while 412 (32.3) articles were from the Washington Post (Table 3).

Table 3. Number of articles by news source		
Source	Number of articles	Percent (%)
New York Times	865	67.7
Washington Post	412	32.3
Total	1277	100

Prominence was defined earlier as a composite variable that includes the total number of news articles, the length of coverage, the position of stories within the newspaper issue, and the presence of supplementary graphic devices in the coverage of a foreign country. Table 4 shows the breakdown of these four prominence indicators by country. The second column of Table 4 shows total number of articles and number of sampled articles in parenthesis. There is a huge variance in total number of articles between countries during the study period: from 30 (Nigeria), the fewest, to 479 (China), the most number of stories. Each sample article was also coded for the following variables: (1) the length of the article (the number of words in a story), (2) the position of the article within the publication (3 = front page; 2 = section front page; 1 = other pages), and (3) the use of supplementary graphic devices (1 = one or more graphic device used; 0 = none). The mean of length, the mean of position, and the ratio of supplementary graphic devices are presented in Table 5.

In terms of length, stories that are Iran, Argentina, Russia, Pakistan, and Israel were prominently reported with more than 850 words per article on the average. This was followed by India, with 820 words. The articles regarding Germany were the shortest, with an average of 326 words per article. Egypt had 420 words per article, and France had around 480 words. In terms of position, articles about Germany were the most prominently displayed (1.49). Israel (1.48), Argentina (1.47), and Afghanistan (1.46) were also more likely to appear in visible positions than other countries. Table 4 presents that Egypt, Nigeria, and Turkey registered a position mean of 1.00, which means that articles about these countries mostly appeared in less visible pages rather than in the front or section front pages. Stories about South Korea noticeably ranked at the top (0.57) in their use of graphic devices, followed by South Africa (0.55), Japan (0.43), and Turkey (0.42). Almost half of the articles regarding these countries had supplementary graphic devices. Article dealing with Iran, Iraq, and Saudi Arabia barely employed supplementary graphic devices (Table 4).

Table 4. News prominence of the countries

Country	Total number of articles (Number of sampled articles)	Mean length	Mean position	Ratio of graphic device
Afghanistan	207 (61)	730	1.46	0.23
Argentina	191 (57)	860	1.47	0.3
Brazil	125 (40)	610	1.43	0.28

Canada	201 (55)	541	1.42	0.22
China	479 (138)	761	1.38	0.28
Colombia	109 (32)	691	1.16	0.25
Egypt	42 (13)	420	1	0.38
France	193 (60)	477	1.33	0.37
Germany	186 (53)	326	1.49	0.4
Great Britain	245 (69)	512	1.25	0.25
India	273 (73)	820	1.29	0.34
Iran	94 (30)	872	1.17	0.13
Iraq	158 (40)	663	1.18	0.13
Israel	393 (130)	850	1.48	0.25
Japan	368 (119)	758	1.39	0.43
Mexico	183 (48)	702	1.25	0.33
Nigeria	30 (11)	499	1	0.18
Pakistan	268 (72)	851	1.43	0.35
Russia	238 (76)	856	1.36	0.26
Saudi Arabia	45 (15)	605	1.07	0.13
South Africa	39 (11)	717	1.27	0.55
South Korea	76 (23)	627	1.43	0.57
Taiwan	77 (27)	616	1.33	0.26
Turkey	82 (24)	599	1	0.42
Total	4302 (1277)	702	1.35	0.3

* Mean length was calculated by the sum of length divided by the number of sampled articles (N).
* Mean position was calculated by the sum of position factor divided by N
* Ratio of graphic device was calculated by the frequency of graphic devices divided by N.

Table 5 presents how positively or negatively each country was portrayed in the newspapers in terms of the percentage of positive and negative articles. The table shows that South Korea, Turkey, South Africa, and Russia had relatively high percentages of positive articles, each registering greater than 40%. On the other hand, Iraq, Iran, Argentina, Pakistan, Colombia, and Israel were presented more negatively than other countries. The percentage of negative articles was greater than 50% for these countries. Iraq was described most negatively. It was ranked at the top in terms of the percentage of negative articles (67.5%) and at the second-bottom in terms of the percentage of positive articles (10.0%).

Valence proportion, or the ratio of the number of positive articles to the number of negative articles, was calculated. This number provides an index that excludes neutral and non-available articles. As Table 5 shows, Canada (2.40) has the highest valence proportion, followed by South Korea (1.71), Great Britain (1.62), Turkey (1.57), and Russia (1.48). Iraq , Colombia, and Iran had the lowest valence proportions, 0.15, 0.19, and 0.32, respectively. In addition, France (.33), India (.34), Israel (.35), Afghanistan (.37), Argentina (.37), and Pakistan (.39) were likely to be portrayed more negatively.

Hypotheses testing

Structural equation modelling using the SPSS program was planned to test the hypotheses and the research question. However, because of limited sample size, SEM analysis produced errors such as negative variances and inadmissible parameter solutions.

Table 5. News valence of countries						
Country	N	Number of positive articles (%)	Number of negative articles (%)	Number of neutral articles (%)	NA	Valence proportion
Afghanistan	61	10 (16.4%)	27 (44.3%)	20 (32.8%)	4 (6.6%)	0.37
Argentina	57	13 (22.8%)	35 (61.4%)	8 (14.0%)	1 (1.8%)	0.37
Brazil	40	14 (35.0%)	15 (37.5%)	10 (25.0%)	1 (2.5%)	0.93
Canada	55	24 (43.6%)	10 (18.2%)	21 (38.2%)	0 (0.0%)	2.4
China	138	25 (18.1%)	61 (44.2%)	48 (34.8%)	4 (2.9%)	0.41
Colombia	32	3 (9.4%)	16 (50.0%)	11 (34.4%)	2 (6.2%)	0.19
Egypt	13	4 (30.8%)	3 (23.1%)	5 (38.5%)	1 (7.7%)	1.33
France	60	7 (11.7%)	21 (35.0%)	30 (50.0%)	2 (3.3%)	0.33

Germany	53	13 (24.5%)	23 (43.4%)	16 (30.2%)	1 (1.9%)	0.57
Great Britain	69	21 (30.4%)	13 (18.8%)	35 (50.7%)	0 (0.0%)	1.62
India	73	12 (16.4%)	35 (47.9%)	25 (34.2%)	1 (1.4%)	0.34
Iran	30	6 (20.0%)	19 (63.3%)	5 (16.7%)	0 (0.0%)	0.32
Iraq	40	4 (10.0%)	27 (67.5%)	9 (22.5%)	0 (0.0%)	0.15
Israel	130	23 (17.7%)	65 (50.0%)	37 (28.5%)	5 (3.8%)	0.35
Japan	119	31 (26.1%)	53 (44.5%)	35 (29.4%)	0 (0.0%)	0.58
Mexico	48	15 (31.3%)	18 (37.5%)	14 (29.2%)	1 (2.1%)	0.83
Nigeria	11	3 (27.3%)	5 (45.5%)	3 (27.3%)	0 (0.0%)	0.6
Pakistan	72	14 (19.4%)	36 (50.0%)	22 (30.6%)	0 (0.0%)	0.39
Russia	76	31 (40.8%)	21 (27.6%)	23 (30.3%)	1 (1.3%)	1.48
Saudi Arabia	15	4 (26.7%)	7 (46.7%)	4 (26.7%)	0 (0.0%)	0.57

South Africa	11	5 (45.5%)	5 (45.5%)	1 (9.1%)	0 (0.0%)	1
South Korea	23	12 (52.2%)	7 (30.4%)	3 (13.0%)	1 (4.3%)	1.71
Taiwan	27	5 (18.5%)	11 (40.7%)	10 (37.0%)	1 (3.7%)	0.45
Turkey	24	11 (45.8%)	7 (29.2%)	6 (25.0%)	0 (0.0%)	1.57
Total	1277	310 (24.3%)	540 (42.3%)	401 (31.4%)	26 (2.0%)	0.57

* Percentages in parenthesis were calculated by the number of positive/negative/neutral articles divided by total number of articles (N).

* NA denotes news articles that were not coded for valence because the articles did not have text but rather a graphic device.

* Valence proportion was calculated as the number of positive articles divided by the number of negative articles.

Therefore, multivariate regression analysis using SPSS was applied to test hypotheses assuming the relationships among variables. The first set of hypotheses proposed the international public relations efforts of a foreign country will influence the U.S. news coverage in terms of the prominence and valence. Multiple linear regressions were calculated to predict each prominence variable (total number of article, length, position, and graphic use) and valence variable (percentage of positive articles, percentage of negative articles, and valence proportion) based on two international PR variables (number of PR contracts and dollar amount of PR contracts). As Table 6 shows, two international PR variables explained 6.5 percent of variance in total number of articles, 12.1 percent of variance in length of the articles, 3.0 percent of variance in position of the articles, and 4.2 percent of variance in graphic use in the articles, and these results were not statistically significant. Neither number of PR contracts nor dollar amount of PR contracts can account for the variance of four prominence variables in a significant level.

Table 6. Regression analysis of international PR variables on news prominence and valence			
Dependent variables	Independent variables		Total R²
	Number of PR contracts	Amount of PR contract prices	
News prominence			
Total number of articles	0.316	-0.155	0.065
Length	0.329	.-422	0.121
Position	-0.012	-0.165	0.03
Graphic use	0.206	0.001	0.042
News valence			
Percentage of positive articles	0.142	-0.011	0.018
Percentage of negative articles	0.116	-0.347	0.086
Valence proportion	-0.009	0.12	0.013
*p<.10; **p<.05; ***p<.01.			
Note. Numbers in the second and third column are standardized coefficient beta.			

Two international PR variables also did not contribute to each of three valence variables. Only tiny portion of variances were explained by two international PR variables, and the all of them were not statistically meaningful: 1.8% of percentage of positive articles; 8.6% of percentage of negative articles; and 1.3% of valence proportion (Table 6). In sum, two international PR variables do not influence any of valence indicators at a significant level. The second set of hypotheses assumed that the extent to which a foreign country is prominently and positively portrayed in the U.S. news media will affect how American public perceive the foreign country.

Table 7 indicates that four news prominence variables were found to explain 31.2% of the variance in public's perceived significance, but was not at a significant level. Among four independent variables, however, total number of articles was turned out as a statistically significant determinant with a **standardized beta of .514.**

Table 7. Regression analysis of news prominence and valence on the public perceptions		
Dependent variables	Independent variables	
	Public's perceived significance	Public feelings
News prominence		
Total number of articles	.514*	-
Length	0.071	-
Position	-0.057	-
Graphic use	-0.18	-
Total R2	0.312	-
News valence		

Percentage of positive articles	-	-0.048
Percentage of negative articles	-	-.589*
Valence proportion	-	0.146
Total R²	-	.468***
*p<.10; **p<.05; ***p<.01.		
Note. Numbers in the second and third column except total R2 scores are standardized coefficient beta.		

On the other hand, according to Table 7, a multiple linear regression shows that three news valence variables explain almost half of the variance in public feelings (46.8%) at the .005 level. Percentage of negative articles was the most powerful determinant to explain differences in public feelings (standardized beta=-.589). Therefore, the results support the hypothesis that the more negatively a foreign country is portrayed in the U.S. news media, the more negatively the country will be perceived by the U.S. public.

The third set of hypotheses suggested that the international public relations efforts of a foreign country will influence U.S. public perception. However, the results indicated that neither of international PR variables did contribute to public's perceived significance and public feelings in a meaningful extent at a significant level; 9.3% of variance in public's perceived significance and 11.3% of variance in public feelings can be accounted for number of PR contracts and dollar amount of the contracts (Table 8).

Model fitting

Because of limited sample size (N=24), test of proposed model fitness was restricted. Compared to the number of parameters to be estimated in the proposed model, 24 cases were not sufficient for the SEM analysis. The result of analysis therefore caused some errors such as negative variance and inadmissible parameter solution. Because this problem could not be solved until more sample cases are collected, a model was modified in a way which decreases the number of indicators. Instead of two latent variables – news prominence and valence - and seven observed indicators linked with these two latent variables, one observed indicator for each latent variable was selected – total number of articles and percentage of negative articles - which was found out to best explain the relationships between variables through previous multiple regression analyses. Figure 4 shows the outcomes of the modified model fitting.

Table 8. Regression analysis of international PR on the public perceptions		
Dependent variables	Independent variables	
	Public's perceived significance	Public feelings
International PR		
Number of PR	0.289	0.05

contracts		
Amount of PR contract prices	0.026	0.303
Total R2	0.093	0.113

*p<.10; **p<.05; ***p<.01.

Note. Numbers in the second and third column except total R2 scores are standardized coefficient beta.

In this modified model, there is one latent variable, or international PR. Two observed indicators – number of PR contracts and amount of PR contract prices - were used for the unobserved latent variable, and squared multiple correlations (SMCs) were used to test the reliability of the observed indicators. Two international PR indicators were reported to have .652 and .548 score, which means that 65.2% and 54.8% of the observed indicators were explained by the latent variables (i.e., international PR).

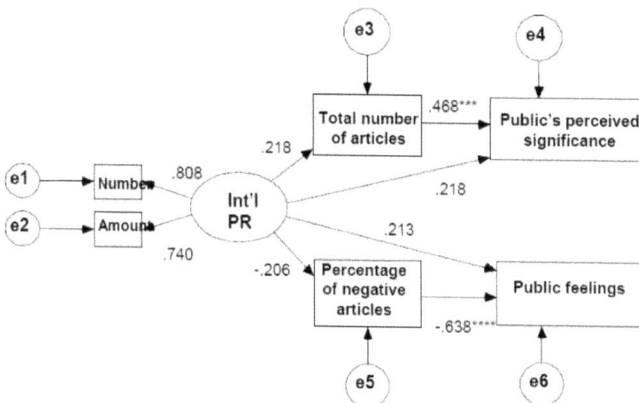

Figure 4. Modified model fitting
*p<.10; **p<.05; ***p<.01; ****p<.001.

The standardized regression weight from total number of articles to public's perceived significance is .468 [critical ratio (CR) = 2.589] and is statistically significant (p<.01), and the regression weight from percentage of negative articles to public feelings is -.638 (CR=-4.181, p<.001). The results of model testing support two hypotheses: the more often a country is reported in the news, the more significantly the country is perceived by the U.S. public (H2-a); the more negatively a country is portrayed in the news, the more negatively the country is perceived by the public (H2-b).

The relationships between international PR efforts and news coverage were not statistically significant (H1-a and H1-b). The amount of international PR efforts was significantly related neither to total number of articles (standardized regression weight =.218, CR=.901, p=.357) nor to percentage of negative articles (standardized regression weight =-.206, CR=-.850, p=.395).

Table 9. Estimates of model testing				
Parameters	**Model**			
	Unstandardized	**SE**	**CR**	**Std.**
Regression Weights				
PR → Total number of articles	0.016	0.017	0.901	0.218
PR → Percentage of negative articles	0	0	-0.85	-0.206
PR → Amount of PR contract prices	1			0.74
PR → Number of PR contracts	0.002	0.001	1.858	0.808
PR → Public's perceived significance	0.002	0.002	1.016	0.218
PR → Public feelings	0.002	0.002	1.159	0.213
Total number of articles → Public's perceived significance	0.062	0.024	2.589***	0.468
Percentage of negative articles → Public feelings	-70.028	16.749	-4.181***	-0.638
Variance				
PR		261699 0.696	181466	1.442

		4	
e1	4.995	4.9 05	3.33 9*** *
e2	216106 2.796	145 602 7	3.34 4*** *
e3	12786. 877	382 9.9 72	1.48 4
e4	161.08 5	48. 541	1.01 8
e5	15	0.0 05	3.31 9*** *
e6	94.362	28. 648	3.29 4*** *

Note. SE = Standard Error; CR = Critical Ratio

Chi-square(7) = 10.869, p=.144; GFI=.880; AGFI=.639; NFI=.767; TLI=.738; CFI=.878; RMSEA=.155.

*p<.10; **p<.05; ***p<.01; ****p<.001.

Lastly, as for the direct causal relationships between international PR efforts and public perceptions (H3-a and H3-b), there is no statistical evidence to show the influence of international PR efforts on the public's perceived significance of foreign countries (standardized regression weight =.218, CR=1.016, p=.309) or on public feelings (standardized regression weight =.213, CR=1.159, p=.247). In addition, the model fit indexes show that collected data do not fit for the proposed model [Chi-square (df=7) = 10.869, goodness-of-fit index (GFI)

= .880, adjusted goodness-of-fit index (AGFI) = .639]. Generally, the model is considered acceptable when GFI is greater than .9 and AGFI is greater than .8. Because these two measures failed to meet these criteria, the suggested model is not acceptable to explain the data. Detailed statistics regarding the tested model are provided in Table 9.

Conceptualization-1 Public Diplomacy:
- Evolution to Modern Diplomacy

The first understanding of public diplomacy suggests that it is simply the current form of a practice that exists in a constant state of fluctuation - the modem manifestation of a profession that is a product of the times rather than one that operates according to a set of unchanging principles. Certainly any study of diplomatic practice must consider the historical evolution of the discipline, but in the context of public diplomacy, it is the perception that this argument is sufficient, rather than simply necessary, to describe public diplomacy that sets it apart from the other two conceptualizations. As Robert F. Delaney says in the introduction of International Communication and the New Diplomacy, "In a sense, public diplomacy is at least as old as Moses' successful attempts to influence the Pharaoh by pressuring his subjects." Indeed, examples abound of leaders and diplomats who recognized the potential advantage of speaking directly to a country's constituents.

As Charles F. Doran and Joel J. Sokolsky noted, even practitioners of classical diplomacy like Otto von Bismarck were known to incorporate elements of public diplomacy: Bismarck altered the Ems Dispatch and leaked the results to the newspapers so as to inflame public opinion in France. However, its most famous proponent, Sir Harold Nicolson, still best defines classical or Renaissance diplomacy: It was courteous, and dignified; it was continuous and gradual; it attached importance to knowledge and experience; it took account of the realities of existing power; and it defined good faith, lucidity and precision as the qualities essential to any sound negotiation.

Nicolson also explicitly stated that in the old diplomacy, "sound negotiation must be continuous and confidential. It was a principle essentially different from that governing the itinerant public conferences with which we have become so familiar since 1919." The 1919 change that Nicolson lamented was "the permanent state of conference introduced by the League [of Nations] system and later by the United Nations." Exemplified by U.S. President Woodrow Wilson's call for "open covenants of peace openly arrived at," and his insistence that "diplomacy should always proceed frankly and in the public view," Nicolson identified this new diplomacy as "open, democratic, multilateral, principled, idealistic, and accomplished by the many small states." However, he also condemned the new diplomacy, saying it "diminishes the utility of professional diplomatists and,.. .[it]

entails much publicity, many rumours, and wide speculation, in that [it] tempts politicians to achieve quick, spectacular, and often fictitious results.. .." Secret meetings between top official were still common, but, as Wilson suggested, constituents were beginning to demand access to the diplomatic activities of their elected officials, and these officials were beginning to recognize the utility of diplomacy "in the public view."

Propaganda in International Relations

One of the most interesting ways in which the practice of diplomacy has focused on the impact of domestic public opinion on a foreign state has been through the use of propaganda as an instrument of foreign policy. As K J. Holsti noted in International Politics: A Framework for Analysis, "With the development of mass politics.. .and a widening scope of private contacts between people of different nationalities, the psychological and public opinion dimensions of foreign policy have become increasingly important."

As he said, insofar as people play a role in determining policy objectives, they become a target of persuasion. Before examining Canada's use of propaganda, this contentious term must be defined. Once again borrowing from Holsti, Terence Qualter provides a comprehensive definition. He suggests that propaganda is: .. .the deliberate attempt by some individual or group to form, control, or alter the attitudes of other groups by the use of the instruments of communication, with the intention that in any given situation the reaction of those so influenced will be that desired by the propagandist.... In the phrase 'the deliberate attempt' lies the key to the idea of propaganda. This is the one thing that marks propaganda from non-propaganda. ... It seems clear, therefore, that any act of promotion can be propaganda only if and when it becomes part of a deliberate campaign to induce action through the control of attitudes [emphasis added][56].

Holsti noted that most definitions of propaganda share four common elements: (1) a communicator with the intention of changing attitudes, opinions and behaviour of others, (2) the symbols - written, spoken or behavioural - used by the communicator, (3) the media of communication, and (4) the audience, or, as it is often called in the terminology of public opinion studies, the 'target.'24 The following section demonstrates that these four elements have appeared several times in specific Canadian policies, most notably in several policies targeting the United States. James Eayrs succinctly summarized Canada's use of propaganda in his 1961 book The Art of the Possible: Government and Foreign Policy in Canada. In this book, Eayrs stated

---

[56] Duchemin, Michael Dean. "New Deal Cowboy: Gene Autry and Public Diplomacy." Order No. 3523669, University of Nevada, Las Vegas, 2012. In PROQUESTMS ProQuest Dissertations & Theses Full Text, http://search.proquest.com/docview/1038158542?accountid=12085.

that an important contradiction existed between public approval for, and Canada's actual use of, propaganda:

> Notwithstanding.. .inhibitions against using propaganda to influence the foreign policies of other states, Canadians have been quite ready to accept it for another and, as they conceive it, a more innocuous purpose, creating a climate of opinion abroad in which Canadian interests could blossom and prosper.

In his 1961 book, Eayrs stated that "In this diluted version, often described as 'publicity' so as to avoid a more offensive if more accurate connotation, propaganda has become an accepted form of governmental activity."26 He noted that Canada's first use of propaganda was to attract foreign immigration and international trade, and, in both World War I and World War n, Canada actively engaged in propaganda in the United States to "enlist American sympathy for the Allied cause." As Eayrs noted, this 1918 campaign, which centred on public lectures to the American public, marked the first time the Canadian government had "used propaganda for the purpose of achieving a political objective of external policy as distinct from commercial advantage." Early in World War n, Prime Minister Mackenzie King rejected this policy, but by 1941, he had repealed his original position, as by that time, even the American President himself was urging Canadian representatives to publicize the war effort in the U.S57.

In 1942, Canada formalized its use of propaganda in the U.S. by creating the Wartime Information Board (WIB). This Privy Council agency was charged with ensuring that "accurate information was available in the United States" to decrease the "danger of misunderstandings" during wartime. Its activities included the distribution of news stories throughout the U.S., assisting in the preparation of articles for American journalists, replying to inquiries for information on the war effort, and disseminating Canadian news around the world. As Eayrs noted, the use of the term propaganda in reference to the activities of the WIB was actively avoided, as the term maintained its "unfavourable connotations." Revisiting Holsti's four-part definition, the WIB lacked the "deliberate campaign to induce action," typical of propaganda, but nonetheless, there was concern in Ottawa that its activities might be interpreted as propaganda[58].

---

[57] Dempsey, Michael Matthew. "Champion of Two Worlds: A Phenomenological Investigation of North Carolina Early College Liaisons' Leadership Experiences." Order No. 3588961, Western Carolina University, 2013. In PROQUESTMS ProQuest Dissertations & Theses Full Text, http://search.proquest.com/docview/1428738850?accountid=12085.

[58] Cole, Randy Edward, Jr. "The Rhetorical Turn in United States Diplomacy Praxis: Public Diplomacy 2.0." Order No. 3557833, Duquesne University, 2013. In PROQUESTMS ProQuest Dissertations & Theses Full Text, http://search.proquest.com/docview/1346683978?accountid=12085.

In the post-war period, the Canadian Information System (CIS) replaced the WEB, and under the direction of the Canadian government, "confined itself to the task of providing more or less factual information about Canada for overseas governments and publics." By 1947, the CIS had been incorporated directly into the Department of External Affairs, and it soon became little more than the department's press office. Canada's only remaining propaganda activity was the International Service of the Canadian Broadcasting Corporation (CBC-IS), which began broadcasting in February of 1945 from the Tantramar Marshes in Sackville, New Brunswick. As Eayrs has reported, initially "the emphasis [of the CBC-IS] was solely upon projecting a picture of Canadian life with special reference to social, cultural, and economic development." However, after the Communists seized power in Czechoslovakia, special targeted broadcasts in Czech and Slovak promoted the aims and policies of the Western democratic powers in an effort to combat communist ideology and Soviet imperialism. Thus, the CBC-IS retained a limited, but distinct, element of propaganda. By the 1970s, the main operational policy of the CBC-IS (renamed Radio Canada International or RCI) was to "convey Canadian identity" to the world. However, the agency was progressively cut back, and, in 1996, nearly folded completely. A revival spurred by federal reinvestment in 1998 prompted some observers to suggest that the Canadian government had recognized that "in an information universe exploding with new media sites every day, quality - measured in availability, attractiveness, ease of use, feedback, and reliability - would be a key factor in Canada's voice being heard abroad."

The propaganda function of RCI today is nowhere near as significant as that of the WEB during World War II, but its continuing existence suggests that the Canadian government continues to believe in the importance of maintaining this capability to spread targeted and deliberate messages to audiences overseas. As KJ. Holsti notes, governments are "quite convinced that diplomatic positions need to be buttressed by favourable foreign attitudes." Or, in other words, "in an era when popular attitudes and behaviour can vitally affect diplomatic relations between states, the use of psychological instruments of policy will become increasingly important for creating the framework of attitudes in which responsiveness grows.. .." It appears that the Canadian experience with propaganda includes many relevant lessons for modem proponents of public diplomacy, and in fact Canada may have already incorporated the tactics and strategies of this policy under a different name: propaganda[59].

---

[59] Berkout, Olga Vadymovna. "Impact of Relationship Context on Evaluations of the Sexual Behavior of Men and Women." Order No. 1495765, The University of Mississippi, 2011. In PROQUESTMS ProQuest Dissertations & Theses Full Text, http://search.proquest.com/docview/880487761?accountid=120 85.

Conceptual Convergence between Public Relations and Public Diplomacy Behaviour

Some time ago a universe of partnerships was barely equivalent to a universe of national states. Similarly, public relations were seldom compared to public diplomacy. When it was, both were lumped together as either "unrefined promulgation" or "complex purposeful publicity" as exemplified in Kunczik (1997) and Manheim (1994). On the other hand, the centre was on stand out perspective, the propagandistic or powerful part of the two correspondences rehearses.

Social obligation starts to exist out of distinguishment that people and enterprises have a moral commitment to all parts of society on the grounds that all individuals are interconnected to one another inside the same group[60]. Thus, morals in public diplomacy ought to additionally incorporate the extraordinary good thinking of worldwide obligation: An administration or state ought to have a moral commitment to all people past its fringes. As Pratt (1989) examined, the progression of human

[60] Roszkowski, Anna. "United Nations Peacekeeping as an International Tool for the Maintenance of International Peace and Security: Has it Exceeded its Original Purpose with the Missions being Carried Out Today?" Order No. 1492871, Webster University, 2011. In PROQUESTMS ProQuest Dissertations & Theses Full Text, http://search.proquest.com/docview/862990348?accountid=120 85.

internationalism and globalization have made this world a worldwide town in which all individuals are interconnected to the point that each individual's activities can have results on other individuals' lives over their fringes. This is the establishment of worldwide obligation regarding disposal of destitution, philanthropic debacles, and imbalances of various sorts all through the world.

Patrick (2003) alluded to worldwide obligation as cosmopolitan morals as in moral commitment goes past outskirts and serves each human on the planet. Patriot morals compares precisely to the idea of public obligation (constrained obligation regarding the stakeholders), while cosmopolitan morals matches the idea of social obligation (augmented obligation regarding society on the loose). The pertinence and promptness of applying the theoretical and estimation structure for public relations conduct on public diplomacy couldn't be better underscored when the ebb and flow status of public diplomacy exploration is considered. Sadly, the conclusion of public relations examine in 1970s fits contemporary public diplomacy research. Regardless of much consideration and engaging, regulating deal with public diplomacy conduct, minimal genuine attempt has been mounted to conceptualize and measure the conduct. Actually, the public diplomacy writing is loaded with thick, rich, inside and out, and authentic records of a mixed bag of courses in which public diplomacy has been led.

Practically the greater part of the four measurements of public relations conduct is the staple subjects of distinct work in public diplomacy research. The reason, course, and channel measurement of public diplomacy practices have regularly charged much work. With a couple of exemptions, essentially all researchers have committed one or two parts to an exchange of one or two measurements, particularly the reason and bearing measurements. The researchers' standardizing underwriting of a two-way, symmetrical model of public diplomacy over a restricted, unbalanced model infers the parallel of the backing of public relations researchers for the two-way, symmetrical model of public relations[61].

Public diplomacy research, then again, has not created a reasonable and estimation system for public diplomacy conduct. Despite the fact that there have been some ordering plans, for example, Piesert's (1978) four models, they have stayed at the level of preparatory theoretical examination and have not been created into reasonable and estimation systems. To finish up, I conceptualized and measured public diplomacy conduct through an application of the four dimensional reasonable skeleton for public relations conduct and the six-element estimation

[61] Fisk, Matthew Henry. "Paradox of Elitism: Vision, Risk, and Diplomacy in the European Career of Colonel John Trumbull (1756-1843)." Order No. 3559788, University of California, Santa Barbara, 2013. In PROQUESTMS ProQuest Dissertations & Theses Full Text, http://search.proquest.com/docview/1354501667?accountid=12085.

model. Emulating Signitzer and Coombs' (1992) call, I put the hypothetical merging between both circles to observational test in which public diplomacy conduct by international safe havens in Washington, D.C. is depicted by the estimation model. A method for exactly testing the joining is investigating how well the six-component estimation model fits the consulates' public diplomacy conduct.

Excellence in Public Relations

In this section, we introduce the theory of the Excellence of Public Relations as a theory of public relations communication control public diplomacy. Then, outline the theoretical convergence theory and the theory of the superiority of Excellence in Public Diplomacy and go to the conceptualization of excellence in the field of public diplomacy, applying best practices in the field of public relations. I conclude this section by placing a perfect convergence (control) between the two areas for empirical testing.

Theory of Excellence in Public Relations

Several theories of public relations are more fundamental and integral theory of qualification[62]. Before theory, public relations are understood in a broad sense as organizational communication without complex theories about their roles and values of the organization and society. Many theories PR were so myopic that were hardly concerned about the impact of communication programs. In fact, some theories focus on the role of specialists in public relations: Technical vs. Manager (Broom and Smith, 1979; Broom and Dozier, 1990) and other models of social relations. They, however, lacked the large general question that the International Association of Business Communicators (IABC) first performed in the creation of research proposals in 1984: How, why and to what extent the media contribute to achieving the objectives of the organization? To address this issue, J. Grunig and his colleagues created a research group and began a historic program of 15 years of research, the study of excellence, with two guides. Pervy research question, "Efficiency of the question", the question of the relationship between the value of public relations and organizational

---

[62] Guenette, Salam. "Franco-British Diplomatic Relations Transformed? the Socio-Political Impact of the Emigres' Presence in Britain." Order No. MS26421, University of Victoria (Canada), 2013. In PROQUESTMS ProQuest Dissertations & Theses Full Text, http://search.proquest.com/docview/1520225582?accountid=12085.

effectiveness . He asked, as public relations make the organization more effective.

The second issue, also called "Perfection question," asked how to organize the function of public relations and was able to contribute to organizational effectiveness. what are the characteristics of the functions of public relations to make a more effective organization. Because of the general nature and the integration of theory, some theories of social relations have the right to test the theoretical convergence between public relations and public diplomacy. To be effective, the question of the theory adopted approach to the values of competence efficiency of the organization, which is one of the four basic approaches to theories: achieving goals, systems, strategic constituencies and competing values. The focus of the competition takes values difficulty having a single definition of organizational effectiveness. Campbell (1977) identified 30 performance criteria, discuss the viability of denying the effectiveness. It values approach assumes that, depending on the stage of the life cycle of the organization, the set of values in competition with another set of value functions as a level of efficiency. For example, when an organization begins to grow, the values that serves as criteria for the effectiveness of the organization and training of human resources through the cohesion and morale[63]. If these values

---

[63] De Santo, Paola Chiara. ""(Ne) Habeas Corpus": The Body and the Body Politic in the Figures of the Ambassador and the Courtesan in Renaissance Italy." Order No. 3626550, Harvard

are fully implemented, the organization is considered to be effective. However, after the organization was founded as an institution, the value of human resources is no longer the level of efficiency. However, one set of values, such as stability and control on the basis of the information and communication takes place in the previous values set.

In short, the focus of competition values asserts that the organization should include the value of strategic regions and their objectives for the organization to reach the most valuable strategic groups Objectives. Pearce and Robinson (1982) distinguish between strategic management of traditional management processes to the old internal balance or activities with strategies to cope with external factors in the environment. Wheelen and Hunger (1987) deepened the understanding of the environment. They have made an important distinction between the work environment, which is a market and social environment, which includes economic, technological, political and cultural spheres. The theory of strategic management in environmental monitoring and adjusting organizations' mission to the crucial role of public relations in the process[64]. Theories strategic

University, 2014. In PROQUESTMS ProQuest Dissertations & Theses Full Text,
http://search.proquest.com/docview/1557754017?accountid=12 085.
[64] Xing, Yi. "China's Panda Diplomacy: The Power of being Cute." Order No. 1479963, University of Southern California,

management, combined with an emphasis values for competition organizational efficiency, provided the answer to questions of efficiency. Public relations matters when the most effective organization to identify strategic constituencies, that may impose threats and opportunities in achieving the organization's objectives and the construction and quality assurance relationship with constituencies done.

In addition, strategic management theory provides an organizational framework for how to increase excellence in public relations with the concept of strategic management levels (Pearce and Robinson, 1982). Strategic management is carried out at three levels: organizational level, at the level of business and functional level. J. Grunig and Repper (1992) offer a theory of strategic public relations, requiring that public relations should play a dual strategic role, both organizational and functional. It argues that PR function makes the greatest contribution to organizational performance with the participation of in the overall strategic management of the organization-Management issues and strategic programs for public relations management of risk communication.

2010. In PROQUESTMS ProQuest Dissertations & Theses Full Text,
http://search.proquest.com/docview/748221700?accountid=120
85.

Work with the second question Excellency, the study Excellence was first discussed organizational characteristics, departmental and program that are necessary for excellent relations with the public. The researchers identified 14 Features excellent communication based on a comprehensive literature review of the theory of communication, public relations, management, organizational psychology and sociology, social and cognitive psychology, feminist studies, political science, decision making, and culture.

Theoretically characteristics were then put in a larger, more research ever conducted intensive public relations and communication management. In 1990-1991, 5,330 participants (public relations senior managers, managers and employees) in 327 organizations in Canada, the United Kingdom and the United States completed a questionnaire containing more than 1,700 pieces of information that were designed to test the theory. As the second wave of the study, in 1994, 25 of the original 327 organizations participated in the case studies, which were conducted face-to-face and telephone interviews, together with an analysis of documents. Using factor analysis, the researchers analyzed 20 variables representing 14 Perfection features excellent public relations and successfully identified one factor in which 20 variables grouped as the theory of expected[65]. The factor is also consistent

---

[65] Williams, Wanda T. "The Western Hemisphere's Pandora's Box: How Race, Communism, and the Roman Catholic Church

with the theory superiority: Features of the basic knowledge of communication department charged higher than "mutual expectations" about communicating with management, charging higher performance organizational culture. In conjunction with the results of qualitative case studies, several similar characteristics were combined into nine.

Later, the tenth principle Excellent, ethics, in addition to existing principles. Through a case study of public relations Slovene, Vercic et al. Found that ethical principles are an important element of excellent public relations and called for more research on ethics. In addition, Rea (1999) reported that the ethical aspect of the behaviour of public relations grouped with other principles of action. Following are 10 principles of excellence.

1. Participation of public relations in strategic management. Effective organizations are involved in long-term strategic planning for the development of the mission and goals that are appropriate for your environment. Excellent unit for public relations involved in the strategic planning process, helping to recognize the leadership of the public concerned party. Organization, which is engaged in strategic public relations, thus developing a communications

Influenced U.S. Foreign Diplomacy with Duvalier's Haiti, 1969-1971." Order No. 1496472, Morgan State University, 2011. In PROQUESTMS ProQuest Dissertations & Theses Full Text, http://search.proquest.com/docview/881638180?accountid=120 85.

program with strategic stakeholders, both external and internal, which provide greatest threats and opportunities for the organization.

2. Strengthening of public relations of the ruling coalition or direct supervision of senior management. Strategic public relations should be an integral part of the strategic management of the organization as a whole. For that to happen, the department of public relations should be able to practice public relations in accordance with professional principles, not the ideas are often mistaken for the top managers. When PR is allowed, public relations executive high level, as a rule, it becomes part of the ruling coalition. Department of Public Relations Date of entry into force of the Organization in the organizational structure for senior PR manager is part of this powerful group of older or has immediate access to this group.

3. The role of integrated public relations. Many organizations develop more than one Per Unit. These devices are generally historically strategically place, reflecting the most important issues concerning the organization of the functions of public relations, when first developed, such as labour relations, media, donors, governments or interest groups. On the other hand, different departments combined all the functions of public relations in the same department or have a mechanism established to coordinate departments. Only in an integrated PR system it is possible that social relations develop new

communication programs to change the strategic state-which, to be managed strategically.

4. Public relations management function is separated from the other functions. Many organizations are functions of public relations, so that the tool supports other departments, such as marketing, human resources, law, finance splinter. When PR is sublimated to other functions, it may be strategically manage because you cannot move the communication resources of strategic audience to another, depending on the integrated PR can. Public Relations advise all control functions with the problems of communication and public relations, but it should be independent of any of these functions, if this is to let them know.

5. Department of Public Relations chaired by the head, and not the technique. Professional public relations of the two main roles are filled in the organization of a director who is planning a strategic and technical programs recording, editing, producing and publishing. Without a manager to coordinate public relations department of public relations cannot be part of strategic management.

6. Two-way symmetrical model of public relations, PR department an excellent model on my program symmetric bidirectional communication in the other three models, though often combined with two-way symmetrical model of asymmetric model elements in the model of a "mixed motive".

7. Symmetric system of organization is essential for effective governance. Excellent organization of decentralized governance structures that give employees autonomy and allow them to participate in decision-making. They also have a symmetric involvement internal communication system. Symmetrical connection with employees increased job satisfaction, because the objectives included in the employee organization's mission.

8. The Department has the necessary expertise to carry out the administrative function and symmetrical public relations. Excellent department of public relations professionals who have learned the theoretical body of knowledge in the field of public relations. Excellent program are working professionals, people who are not only the body's knowledge, but active participation in professional associations and read professional literature.

9. The diversity is embodied in all requisite variety states that effective organizations have more diversity within the organization and in the environment. Requisite Variety is particularly important in public relations, because the unit is responsible for communicating with different audiences. Thus, a great relationship with the public includes both men and women in all functions and professionals from different ethnic and cultural backgrounds.

10. Ethics. To be effective, the organization must take responsibility for their community and

society, in addition to being cost-effective and efficient in achieving the organization's objectives. Effective organizations have the moral responsibility to communicate with the public, where PR should have the primary responsibility for defining social responsibility, public relations that define this responsibility (pp. 22-25).

These 10 principles of excellence in public relations to address the characteristics of communication programs, the department of public relations and organizations that are doing an excellent relationship with the public. Two principles of ethics and symmetrical bidirectional communication are excellent characteristics of external communication programs, thus, the behaviour of public relations. Bilaterally symmetric model is decomposed into two-dimensional and two-way symmetry behaviour. In addition, the ethical aspects of the behaviour of public relations are the principle of ethics.

EU Public Diplomacy Structure and Practice

Acknowledging the confusion and lack of knowledge that exists about its policies and activities, the EU it taking active steps to employ public diplomacy as the mechanism through which it harnesses its smart power to better present itself to the world. It exhibits an awareness of the changing nature of communication with foreign publics and its leaders freely disclosing this, seeking to expand the EU's image beyond its cultural capital. The EU has a complex network of institutions through which it carries out various public diplomacy strategies. The following will outline and highlight the main state-based mechanisms of public diplomacy and some of their most visible activities, followed by a focus on the EU's public diplomacy in the U.S.[66]

It must be noted that the use of the term public diplomacy is rather a new phenomenon for the EU. Observers and scholars have noted that the concept of public diplomacy was not employed or recognized among EU officials or communication materials in the recent past. Perusal of the EU website finds no mention of the term. However, the EU's methods are in line with common perceptions of public diplomacy and EU leaders, aware as always of the changing discourse on international relations, especially in the U.S., have begun to employ the term more readily. The EU is actively involved in new public diplomacy, moving away from the one-way communication model, often seen as propaganda, and toward two-way communication, seeking to engage publics.

According to Benita Ferrero-Waldner, European Commissioner for External Relations and European Neighbourhood Policy, "Public diplomacy

[66] Touloumi, Olga. "Architectures of Global Communication: Psychoacoustics, Acoustic Space, and the Total Environment, 1941-1970." Order No. 3627231, Harvard University, 2014. In PROQUESTMS ProQuest Dissertations & Theses Full Text, http://search.proquest.com/docview/1557745167?accountid=12085.

encompasses all activities which have an impact on the perceptions and the public opinion in third countries about the country or institution engaging in public diplomacy. They are therefore not only aimed at the media and the political actors of third countries but at their societies at large." The EU stresses that EU public diplomacy is "not for domestic consumption" and must be seen as separate from its communication with its members. This, naturally, leads to some confusion because the definition of domestic is not understood by all in the EU to mean internal to the union, as their fellow member countries are still considered foreign. The EU, aware that its own citizens also serve as public diplomacy disseminators, engages in extensive internal communications efforts, linked to its external communications, to inform and educate its member citizens, on the same level as non-EU publics, to eliminate confusion.

The EU's aim is to tackle the sentiment expressed by Madeleine Albright that 'To understand Europe you have to be a genius. This is accomplished by voicing a few, simple messages and answering fundamental questions, such as what defines the EU on the world stage. At the heart of the EU's public diplomacy have been its humanitarian aid to, and trade and cooperation agreements with, non-EU countries. Its recent public diplomacy has been focused on broadening this picture; moving away from the image of its global impact as only "trade and aid," so that global publics recognize its efforts toward economic and human rights reforms in other countries as well.

The European Commission, as the executive body, is responsible for representing the EU to the world. The Commission is composed of departments called Directorate Generals (DGs), of which DG-External Relations (DG RELEX) is tasked with managing relations, including public diplomacy, with countries outside of the EU and international and regional organizations. DG RELEX coordinates the work of the 136 Delegations of the EU around the world. These representations act as the voice of the EU. They promote EU values and interests and their activities, which include printed and digital information materials aimed at the general public, the hosting of events, the operation of information centres, and communications with businesses and media, are similar to those of embassies. Because of the difference in sizes and resources of each of the Delegations, as well as the difference of circumstances of the third countries, it is difficult to speak in narrow terms of Delegations' varied activities. Other DGs also participate in the EU's international communication. These include ECHO, Development, Enlargement, Trade and ECFIN, who have their own information and communication units[67].

---

[67] Ripley, Charles. "Pathways to Peace, Progress, and Public Goods: Rethinking Regional Hegemony." Order No. 3559641, Arizona State University, 2013. In PROQUESTMS ProQuest Dissertations & Theses Full Text, http://search.proquest.com/docview/1353674019?accountid=12

The Europe Aid Cooperation Office (DG ECHO) is responsible for implementing external aid programs and projects across the world. The mission of its communications is to promote the EU's extensive humanitarian aid, for which it allots 0.5-3 percent from every aid contract. The DG Development and Relations with African, Caribbean and Pacific States devises the EU's development policy for all developing countries and coordinates political relations with sub-Saharan Africa, the Caribbean and the Pacific (ACP), the African Union, regional economic communities, and the overseas countries and territories in all the areas for which it is responsible. It is imbued with a great deal of soft power stemming from the EU's large amounts of humanitarian aid to developing countries. In 2005 it launched the campaign "Europe Cares" to publicize its efforts in support of the Millennium Development Goals.

The DG Enlargement is responsible for the expansion process of the EU, carrying out the implementation of enlargement policies. Within the framework of the Communication Strategy for Enlargement, it communicates with and about candidate and potential candidate countries, as well as EU citizens, to promote the benefits of enlargement. It uses the mediums of EUROPA, the official European Union website, as well as EU Tube, the Commission's official You Tube channel,

085.

the TV service "Europe by Satellite," and the question and answer service Europe Direct.60 This DG has obvious public diplomacy potential through its work dealing with the prospect of EU ascension. DG Trade promotes the EU's interests through the EU's trade policy. Its international communications arise out of negotiations on bilateral and multi-lateral trade agreements.

The DG for Economic and Financial Affairs' (DG ECFIN) mission is to improve the economic wellbeing of the citizens of the EU, by developing and promoting policies that lead to sustainable economic growth, a high level of employment, stable public finances and financial stability. It concentrates its communication resources on the financial centres of Washington, DC, Tokyo, Singapore, New York, and Kuala Lumpur, where its representatives organize conferences on issues relating to the Euro. Since the entry into force of the Lisbon Treaty, the newly created position of High Representative for the Union in Foreign Affairs and Security Policy, or Foreign Minister, also serves as the Vice-President of the Commission. The current representative, Catherine Ashton, serves as the coordinator and representative of the Common Foreign and Security Policy and is expected to increase the visibility and impact of the EU.

Also, under the auspices of the Treaty, the DG Development, the DG Enlargement, the DG Trade and ECHO come under the jurisdiction of the newly created European External Action Service

(EEAS), which will serve as the Foreign Office for the EU. The EEAS is intended to present the voice and implement the foreign policy of the EU in a more coherent and unified way. The EEAS will coordinate national foreign ministries and diplomatic corps in support of EU policies and communicate with foreign governments in bilateral negotiations. The new organization, under the direction of the new Foreign Minister, will also take responsibility for the EU's delegations around the world. The EEAS is expected to help the EU in a number of ways, including, consolidating its foreign policy, increasing its global influence, and helping those member states not large enough to have their own embassies.

In addition to the appeal of ascension into the union, the EU extends its other smart power mechanisms to strike up partnerships with neighbouring countries outside of the EU. One such public diplomacy endeavour is the European Neighbourhood Policy (ENP), developed in 2004, to strengthen and build positive relationships with the EU's neighbouring countries. The central elements of the ENP are the bilateral ENP Action Plans agreed to between the EU and each of the 16 partners, which build upon a mutual commitment to the common values of democracy and human rights, rule of law, good governance, market economy principles and sustainable development[68].

---

[68] Khakimova, Leysan. "An Exploratory Study of the Meaning of Public Diplomacy: Network Approach." Order No. 3599613, University of Maryland, College Park, 2013. In

Similar to the requirements the EU demands of its candidate states, it also uses its prestige and positive image in the world to enact reforms among its neighbours, with the incentive of becoming a partner through the ENP. In the realm of the ENP, its public diplomacy focuses on fostering ties with neighbourhood country publics by relaxing travel restrictions for certain categories of the population, instituting exchange programs for students, and scholars and the building of networks between different civil society groups. In this way, the EU ensures the spread of its values and ideas throughout the European continent and beyond. Another similar program of note is the Euro-Med Partnership, which provides for a dynamic and comprehensive relationship along the lines of politics, economics, culture, environment and society between the EU and its 15 partners from the Southern Mediterranean and the Middle East.

It has its own ENPI Information and Communication Support Project, launched by the European Commission in January 2009, to bring awareness to the relationship between the EU and its Euro-Med partners. The EU does a great deal of work in people-to-people communication and exchanges through its European Union Visitors Program (EUVP), which brings young professionals and future leaders from all over the world to the EU so that they may learn first-hand about EU institutions, functions and policies, and foster long-term relationships with their counterparts in the EU. The Erasmus Mundus program, which promotes European higher education, offers grants and scholarships towards educational endeavours, and fosters partnerships with non-EU institutions of higher education. Programs aimed at youth point to a strategic focus on reaching out to future opinion leaders of the world, building understanding early on so as to continue solid relationships into the future.

The EU's Delegation to the U.S, which functions like an embassy, has been in Washington, DC for 50 years, and was granted diplomatic status in 1971. The Delegation's activities cover all major areas of the U.S.–EU relationship, including trade, political, economic and financial, development, agriculture, consumer policy, transport, energy, environment, science and technology, press and media, and communications and public affairs. Its public diplomacy efforts are carried out by a separate Press and Public Diplomacy (PPD) section, currently headed by Anthony Smallwood, Counsellor and Head of Press & Public Diplomacy, who also serves as spokesperson of the Delegation. The PPD section is the only EU Delegation sections in the world to employ the term "public diplomacy" in its title; all other delegations use "public affairs," "press/media," or "information," speaking to the relevance of the term to the U.S. The PPD section informs the U.S. media about the Commission's positions on issues and provides them with information about current developments in the EU. It also monitors the U.S. media and provides information on news and events of interest to the EU. In his 2005 analysis, Fiske De Gouveia wrote,

> ...the delegation has identified four distinct areas of public diplomacy activity: general perception-oriented public diplomacy (e.g. correcting American public misperceptions of contemporary Europe); specific issue public diplomacy (for instance, lobbying for the extension of the US visa waiver scheme to all 25 (now, 27) EU member states); co-operative EU-US public diplomacy (identifying ways of working with the US government on, for example, public diplomacy strategies in the Middle East); competitive and conflictual EU-US public diplomacy (relating to issues of dispute between the EU and US such as the Airbus-Boeing rivalry or lifting of the EU-China arms ban)[69].

Current issues that drive the public diplomacy efforts of the EU Delegation include the strengthening of EU-U.S. trade, dispelling the image of the EU as solely an economic bloc, the promotion of the EU as a leader in the dialogue on climate

[69] Christenson, Joel C. "From Gunboats to Good Neighbors: U.S. Naval Diplomacy in Peru, 1919-1942." Order No. 3571567, West Virginia University, 2013. In PROQUESTMS ProQuest Dissertations & Theses Full Text, http://search.proquest.com/docview/1426846310?accountid=12085.

change and the promotion of its status as one of the world's larger aid donors. Smallwood affirms, as previously stated, that the EU Delegation to the U.S., recognizing the need for communication to be two-way, has moved away from traditional public diplomacy and the role of propaganda disseminator. Public diplomacy is no longer seen as only communication with elites, but as interaction with the public and non-traditional elites, like leaders from non-governmental organizations. Smallwood also points out the EU's recognition of the changing demographics of the U.S. and the need for the EU's public diplomacy activities in the U.S. to project messages differently depending on demographics.

Touching on what many EU observers have opined, Smallwood acknowledges there is awareness that the EU is no longer the dominant power it once was, and that it "can't afford to let history and culture guide relationships always." This is why its U.S. public diplomacy operates with the understanding that there is a "need to invest heavily in understanding each other better." Aside from the media, specific public diplomacy targets identified by the EU Delegation include "next generation leaders" (opinion leaders), with the intent to build relationships.

As well as the standard informational website (www.eurunion.org/eu/) and publications, including magazines EU Focus, "an in-depth treatment of important European issues and the transatlantic relationship" and EU Insight, "a timely EU issue brief with special attention to EU/US relations," the Delegation conducts more pro-active activities, such as regular meetings by the ambassador with members of Congress, students and academics, as well as speaking tours around the nation. The EU's Centres of Excellence, located in universities throughout the U.S., promote the study of the EU and its policies through research, teaching and activities. The Delegation also hosts and organizes, sometimes in partnerships with member state embassies, cultural programs and activities, like Euro Week and the European film festival, and also hosts a year-round internship program for college students. Though publics are often confused about EU policies and decisions, this has not affected public opinion, as its public diplomacy has succeeded in fostering a favourable image. According to a 2005 poll, 41 percent of people in the world had a positive opinion of the EU, while 31 percent were neutral. However, because this image is guided by soft power, the EU is rarely seen as a formidable power in the area of global affairs, which has come to hurt its global standing and crucial international relationships.

Additionally, one survey found a gap between how the EU presents itself and how publics actually see it. The EU is actually not seen "as a 'normative power' exporting universal values of democracy and human rights;" it seems to no longer be regarded "as a social model to be imitated." The EU's long standing role as a cultural behemoth seems to not be enough for it to maintain a leadership role in the world; it is instead viewed as harmless and insignificant.

EU Public Diplomacy in the U.S.

In terms of its public diplomacy in the U.S., the EU has a great comparison at its disposal: some have coined the phrase, the United States of Europe to refer to the EU. This is something EU public diplomacy can use to its advantage to make U.S. publics more aware and informed about the EU's unique structures and attributes; by comparing the two. The EU needs to reorient and reinvent its public diplomacy strategy in a way that highlights its differences from the U.S., which despite differences among member states, is, collectively, a nation state with a common language and history. This will show the American public that the EU is a new and novel entity that must be given due credit and attention, causing them to revaluate their previous assumptions and expectations[70].

Americans clearly like the EU, on account of its culture and history, but view sceptically its role in international affairs. This is why the focus can move away from simply conveying the attraction of the

[70] Carlson, Joana Renee. "Blurring the Boundaries of Cold War Foreign Relations: Popular Diplomacy, Transnationalism, and U.S. Policy Toward Post-Revolutionary China and Cuba." Order No. 3462283, The Florida State University, 2010. In PROQUESTMS ProQuest Dissertations & Theses Full Text, http://search.proquest.com/docview/875962580?accountid=120 85.

EU, though this of course must remain as the underlying principle behind all EU public diplomacy initiatives, and toward fostering greater understanding of the nuances of the EU that make it a model and distinct actor on the global scene. While it is true that all aspects of the EU's complex structure do not need to be known or understood by the U.S.,156 by continuing, and even broadening, the EU's focus on educating the American public about the EU's distinct characteristics in comparison to the U.S., the EU will reinvigorate the interest of the public. This new information and framing will be welcomed after years of traditional fact dissemination in support of the unity rhetoric, which has evidently lost its lustre and has fallen on deaf ears.

At the same time, reiterating the shared values the two partners have, in spite of their institutional and cultural differences, is also needed to cement the relationship on all levels. It is important for Americans, especially since they may not understand certain aspects like the structure or policies of the EU, to be reminded of the shared values of democracy and freedom, economic freedom and respect for human rights they and their European counterparts possess. This would make the EU more relatable and not so foreign. This is something that EU public diplomacy has endeavoured to do, though there is room for expansion. First, presenting the broader shared values in order to establish a connection, then, narrowing down the institutional and structural differences in order to guide Americans away from believing the EU is exactly the same as the U.S., will be helpful in maintaining the respect and positive opinion Americans already have of the EU. Barroso has made allusions to an awareness of this approach in his recent speech, where he mentioned similarities of the EU and the U.S., as well as room for disagreements, pointing out that this was normal[71].

Publics, though they may not understand the nuances of the EU, will be conscious of honesty, because it shows that they are being treated as active partners, who are important to the EU, instead of just the receptors of propaganda. Since Americans have already aware of the EU's stumbles, it is best if the EU comes clean and talks about them openly instead of just glossing over or denying them. Publics will attribute more credibility to the EU for being honest and be more open to hear what it has to say. As for specific public diplomacy efforts, the numerous actions of the EU Delegation to the U.S., as detailed above, are sufficient in educating and maintaining relationships with the public. Future endeavours, however, should convey the aforementioned reframing of the EU's identity. This must be done

---

[71] Yuan, Tian. "The New Great Leap Forward A Two-Case Analysis of Modern China's Efforts in External Communication Strategies." Order No. 1514188, University of Southern California, 2012. In PROQUESTMS ProQuest Dissertations & Theses Full Text, http://search.proquest.com/docview/1027917966?accountid=12085.

with the awareness that such a shift in discourse will take time and will not happen overnight.

With this in mind, there are several changes to the EU Delegation website that can be made to better inform the American public of the EU's identity and better orient them to its shift. The EU Delegation website is comprehensive, thorough and informative, requiring little modification. That being said, there are a few minor additions, cantering on accessibility and the presentation of the EU's distinctiveness, from which it may benefit. The EU Delegation website should be enhanced to be on par with the Europe website, geared toward EU publics, by making it more creative, vibrant and interactive.

The front page is rather cluttered and can have less text, perhaps choosing one prominent aspect to focus on, such as "News," or the "Spotlight" section. It would be advisable to remove the left "Policy Areas" sidebar, as it is already a link at the top. Front page news can also feature more EU-U.S. relations-cantered information, as it is assumed that Americans visiting the site will be more interested by news they can relate to more readily. One page that can be featured more prominently is the "EU in the US Events Calendar - From the 27 EU Member States" page. The inclusion of this page highlights the EU's support and collaboration with its member states and is very effective in educating the public about the EU structure and composition as diverse and all encompassing. The website needs more direct interaction with the public. In line with educating the American public about differences between the EU and the U.S., a simple "Test Your Knowledge" quiz can be placed on the website. In this same respect, although requiring less interaction, and perhaps more attractive to an older audience, would be the addition of a "Fact of the Week/Month" page cantering on some aspect of the EU-U.S. relationship.

Challenges for EU Public Diplomacy

Despite EU public diplomacy's best efforts to enhance the EU's image in the eyes of the American public, as well as increase awareness of and refine its efforts in the realm of global politics, it has failed to completely deliver on its goals. Though public diplomacy tries to combat the global public's confusion and lack of awareness about EU specifics through initiatives of information dissemination, the lack of coherence among the EU's structures and policies serves as a direct adversary. One of the most commented on challenges faced by the EU's public diplomacy is the EU's lack of a unified voice. While public diplomacy touts the EU's efforts at reaching consensus on issues, global media report on the member states' disagreements. In this way, the EU's public diplomacy, much like the EU, is deemed unreliable and confusing, leading to questions about its credibility[72].

---

[72] Zajicek, Taylor Craig. "Modern Friendship: The "New Turkey" and Soviet Cultural Diplomacy, 1933-1934." Order No. 1563149, University of Washington, 2014. In

External communication strategies are hindered by EU problems with consistency, focus and integration, which prevent EU public diplomacy from having a substantial or ever-lasting effect on the hearts and minds of non-EU publics because the union's image, as portrayed to foreign publics, is inconsistent with the picture they see in the media. The multiplicity of EU actors and their lack of consensus on issues have caused many to speculate that this is, and will continue to be, the EU's obstacle to achieving super power status. The EU has presented the opposite of a united front on issues, and this has led to questions about its strength as a global actor; some reducing it to the status of an immature player, which greatly reduces it integrity and impact.95 The member states' allegiance to their national interests over those of the EU, which is often the reason for the lack of consensus, has called into question their commitment to the EU's values and their actual investment in its success. Sometimes member states' position is different from that of the EU on certain issues, which is acceptable in the tenets of the EU, but as this is accepted by outside publics as the stance of the EU, they are left even more confused and critical of the EU's lack of unity.

For example, on the issue of genetically modified crops, the EU has recently allowed for some forms to be cultivated, while France and Greece oppose. Depending on which voice they hear, foreign publics will get a different message, obviously causing confusion and frustration. The EU's inability to forge a coherent and consistent foreign policy serves as a counter to what EU public diplomacy has attempted to convey – a united and decisive global actor. For example, seeking influence in the war in Afghanistan, Germany, France and Britain each claimed to speak for the EU, against the objections of the Belgian Presidency (in 2006) and smaller member states. Because the EU is at times represented by various voices, both state and non-state based, and because there is a lack of a clear designation as to who really represents the EU, calling into question the much-debated concept of European identity, non-EU publics fall victim to incorrect information and information bombardment. In addition to disagreements between members on issues, which negatively affects EU public diplomacy's goal of projecting a unified position, the lack of collaboration between the EU and the member countries' public diplomacy also complicates EU public diplomacy work. As the union is comprised of 27 extremely different countries, there is no doubt that this is the case.

Many of the states, especially the more prosperous ones, have had their own public diplomacy strategies for a number of years. They have become skilled in the practice of public diplomacy and having reaped its benefits, are reluctant to share or give up their information monopolies. This clearly supports the assertion about member states' overarching commitment to national interest, over that of the EU, which, while natural and expected, like their differing positions on issues, does nothing to legitimize EU public diplomacy. It actually discredits the EU's public diplomacy as simply in the business of covering up the EU's true image or trying to silence its individual members. It also shows a lack of awareness and understanding about the benefits of cooperative public diplomacy, like eliminating redundant campaigns or establishing cooperation in other areas. Because of the lack of collaboration on public diplomacy efforts, misunderstandings arise out of confusing the EU's public diplomacy strategy with those of its member states[73].

When non-EU publics are overwhelmed with competing messages, the messages are either all ignored, leading to a complete lack of impact, or, the ones which are most familiar, often times, the ones coming from the individual member states that already engender awareness or have relationships with the public, are accepted. In either case, the EU is the one that suffers and is marginalized. With information already being so plentiful, EU public diplomacy is often trumped by its secondary status to member states' more experienced and already

[73] Yan, Jing. "Is China's Outward FDI Politically Driven?" Order No. 1509015, Georgetown University, 2012. In PROQUESTMS ProQuest Dissertations & Theses Full Text, http://search.proquest.com/docview/1012104278?accountid=12085.

established initiatives. The EU benefits, in terms of soft power, from its members' experience with public diplomacy, which adds to its visibility and ensures a positive global image, while, at the same time, because those members continue to practice their own public diplomacy that of the EU's is ignored, co-opted or misinterpreted.

While general public diplomacy goals, for both the EU and individual members, pertain to the increase of awareness among global publics, more specific goals of member states differ, depending on several factors, including the nation's global standing and relationships. For example, as previously mentioned, a country like Malta, well aware of its attraction as a tourist destination, will focus on this aspect in its public diplomacy, while Romania may perhaps be focused on conveying the image of a new and improved economy. While such images are not detrimental to the EU, they are distracting from the union as a whole, facilitating the foreign publics' continued ignorance of the union, thus perpetuating their confusion out of lack of knowledge.

A reason for the EU members' lack of desire to unify their public diplomacy endeavours may be a flaw in the EU's internal communications, which has also been criticized as insufficient. The number of years it took to ratify the Lisbon Treaty, first devised in 1999 and rejected in referendums by French and Dutch voters in 2005 and Irish voters in 2008, is a testament to this. Clearly, member citizens did not see the need for the reforms the treaty would enact because they were not properly informed of its benefits; or perhaps did not like what they saw. In either case, this portrays to foreign publics an inconsistency in EU policies, as EU publics are not informed or not taken into consideration. The member countries' publics are equally as confused as the non-EU ones, as previously stated, about the EU's identity and policies, as well as their roles and contributions to them.

As Howorth points out, among the current EU member states there are two very different visions of the Union itself. One sees the EU as a project that is explicitly political, with clear strategic objectives, that requires the application of serious political will, the designation of definitive borders and a discernible finality. The other sees it as essentially a process that is primarily commercial and is explicitly apolitical, that is focused on regulatory frameworks and progressive enlargement, with no definitive borders and no sense of finality.

The EU public diplomacy's unsuccessful attempts to foster awareness of its policies in the world are an extension of this same lack of success internally. Whether from lack of trying or lack of action, the EU has not cultivated an understanding and embodiment of a united EU identity among its members. The question of a solitary EU identity is a hotly contested topic, and while this paper does not address the issue, it must be said that the concept of an EU identity is not necessarily separate from a European identity, arising out of continental boundaries, histories and relationships. Because this issue is not addressed by EU public diplomacy, or rather, gets lost amidst its other issues, publics, both EU and non-EU alike, understand it to be in question. Member states continue to push their own agendas with, what seems like, little regard for the implications for their collective EU image.

The EU members' lack of awareness is also seen as a lack of engagement, and therefore, interest in the EU, which in turn negatively shapes non-EU publics' levels of interest and curiosity. On a broader scale, the EU's structure is also blamed for the failure of its public diplomacy in presenting to the public a coherent new voice. The confusions about its institutions and officials previously alluded to prevent any public diplomacy efforts to counteract them. The rotating presidency of the Commission is cited as a major disadvantage for the EU's public diplomacy. The half-yearly change in leaders requires a level of vigilance from non-EU publics which very few are willing to dedicate to, especially since they are already sceptical of the position's benefits for the union. The fact that a different country is given the title of president every few months only continues to enable the critique that individual member states are more apt to favour their own national interest above that of the union.

While EU communication has sought to present the EU institutions to non-EU publics in a simple and comprehensive way, EU headlines override this attempt by featuring stories of the EU's never-ending bureaucratic complexities. Competing with local and global media to correct EU portrayals has been a thorn in the side of EU public diplomacy. The issue of lack of credibility among foreign publics arising out of its relatively new and confusing identity explains the EU's perpetual second place finish in this competition. Additionally, the EU's reliance on soft power is now seen as a hindrance to its attempts at reasserting itself as a major player in international affairs, and, subsequently, to its public diplomacy.

The EU's centuries-old "historical capital" is no longer enough to survive in a world where military powers rule, especially with its demographic decline, energy dependency and lack of key natural resources. With the advent of several wars and an economic crisis, the EU's promotion of culture and language is seen as insignificant and overused. Its public diplomacy requires a contemporary spin, which must include the presentation of the EU as a more powerful union, in terms of collective strength, both as a united and military power. The lack of a collective military force only exacerbates what many deem as the EU's problem.

EU public diplomacy is greatly hindered in this area as its expounding of the benefits of soft power to a public that has witnessed the rise of war is seen as irrelevant and out of touch. The EU member states' disagreements on engagement, and reluctance to get involved, in military operations angers publics, especially those whose countries are actively involved in wars, like the U.S. This perpetuates the opinion of the EU as elitist, weak and, even cowardly, causing publics to lose affinity and interest. EU public diplomacy's promotion of its soft power, in countries whose own internal communication aims at building support among its citizens for their wars is seen as completely contradictory to state aims and is, naturally, ignored, or derided.

CHAPTER 5: DISCUSSION AND ONCLUSION

Main issues

The results of hypotheses testing partially support the propositions of the second level agenda-setting theory. How positively (or negatively) a country is portrayed in the news more influenced how people feel about the country than how prominently a country is reported in the news influenced how significantly the country is perceived by the public. The strong relationship between total number of articles and the public's perceived significance of a country (standardized regression weight =.468) is consistent with the outcomes of Wanta et al.'s study (2004). Wanta et al. (2004) also found that the respondents' affective evaluation was not influenced by positive coverage of a country but by the negative coverage. In the current study, among three indicators of news valence, only percentage of negative articles turned out to be significantly related to public feelings.

The results of this study, however, did not provide statistical evidence to support a direct influence of international PR efforts on either news coverage or public perceptions even though hypothesized directions and decent scores of regression weights were estimated (around .22). The current study also showed that international PR bears a weak indirect effect on public perception of a foreign country, which is mediated by news coverage

(.102 on public's perceived significance; .131 on public feelings). There are some possible explanations why international PR has only limited effects on media and public agenda. Even though only international PR was considered to influence international news content and public perceptions in this study, there are a lot of influential factors to affect news content and public perceptions of foreign countries. This study did not control other substantial factors, and followings may be such factors.

Firstly, historical events during the analysis timeframe may have influenced the news prominence and valence of certain countries in a certain way. For example, the 2002 World Cup and the 2002 Winter Olympics generated a considerable coverage. South Korea made it to the 2002 World Cup semi-finals and co-hosted this international sports event. Its performance and role may have produced a substantially positive coverage of the country. President Clinton's visit to China also produced a heavy positive coverage of China. On the other hand, the "War on terror" launched following September 11, 2001, must have produced a large number of negative articles about Middle Eastern countries. Severe conflicts with guerrillas and terrorist groups, and problems with international drug traffickers in Colombia caused noticeably high percentage of negative articles regarding the country. These historical events may encourage government-driven PR activities, but that does not always happen.

Second, some countries have involved long-lasting economic and political interests with the U.S. China and Russia are such cases, and they tend to be prominently portrayed by the U.S. media and also significantly perceived by the U.S public regardless their PR efforts. In addition, countries which have potential/current conflict with the U.S., especially military involvements, such as Iran, Iraq, Afghanistan, and Pakistan, tend to be considered significant because of potential damage on people's daily life as well as national interest. These countries rarely have PR contracts with U.S. firms, but U.S. publics perceive these countries as significant and U.S. media oftentimes cover these countries in their stories.

These factors – international historical event, economic/political interests with foreign countries, and potential/current threats of foreign countries - are generally regarded as having high news value or news worthiness. Considering that countries or foreign affairs with high news value are likely to be appeared in the news media regardless of the countries' PR efforts, news value is another major determinant to affect news content and public perceptions. Third, there are long-established public perceptions of foreign countries as allies or enemies in relation to the U.S. For example, Canada and Great Britain are traditional U.S. allies, and the favourable opinion about these countries has not been built in a short time. Such a long-established public perception may not be affected by short-term PR activities. Lastly, although this study hypothesized that more international PR effort will lead people to consider the country as significant to the U.S., people in the survey may perceive the term "significant" somewhat differently from what the researcher conceptualized.

A country's significance or vital interest can be considered as two different ways—positive or negative, but it seems that respondents in the CCFR survey were more likely to perceive these terms as negative (e.g., threat to national security) than positive. People tend to connect significance of a country with serious political or economic issues. For example, even if a country like Bahama makes huge PR efforts to promote tourism in the U.S., it is considered as a nice vacation destination, not necessarily as a "significant" country to the U.S. In contrast, countries like Iran and Syria are considered as significant to the U.S. without any PR activities in the U.S. because they are considered as enemies to threaten the U.S. national security. There are some empirical cases to imply the influence of international PR on public perceptions and media coverage.

For example, Japan, Mexico, Saudi Arabia, and South Korea are enjoying high significance among U.S. public with having relatively many contracts with the U.S. PR firms. In spite of the cases which support the potential of international PR, the effect seems to be offset by the other cases mentioned above. This study is one of a few that quantified public relations and tried to find empirical evidence of PR influence on the news media and public perception. International PR efforts was operationally defined and quantified from the publicly available government-generated data. Lee (2004) argued that although the strategic public relations of foreign governments are a strong determinant of international news flows, along with environmental and relational factors, but how PR efforts actually work to achieve their objectives have yet to be critically examined. Even though the FARA dataset has some limitations, it is still the best available source of international PR data. How to improve and utilize this resource remains a challenge to future researchers.

EU Public Relation, Public Diplomacy, and Communication

The advanced search option on the Europa Web site was used to search the keywords: Public relations; public diplomacy; and communication. The search for public relations only provided the Web site for the External Relations. However, when the content of this Web page was examined, it was found that this is only an informative Web page that almost functions like an index for the Europa Web site, pointing visitors to important links about the European Union such as EU institutions, history, treaties, etc. ("External relations," n.d.). Then the keywords public diplomacy and diplomacy were entered into the search box, but this search also provided the Web site of External Relations.

However, I came across with the term public diplomacy while reading another document.

The research question one was answered through secondary analysis of the EU reports on immigrant integration and an examination documents found on the EU Web site related to EU immigrant integration efforts and communication strategies. Based on the research conducted, although there does not seem to be an existing public relations and public diplomacy strategy geared specifically towards Turkish immigrants or towards third country nationals (TCNs) in general, there are EU Commission proposals and strategies developed for actions in this area. The EU institutions, especially the Commission, seem to be aware of the lack of information among the public about the European Union in general. This is evident from all the decisions and proposed actions to enhance relationships with the EU citizens through various initiatives. Also, the Commission argues that EU member states should be better informed to provide relevant and up-to-date information to their citizens about the European Union and its direct influence on their lives. However, the Commission is also aware that establishing partnerships with EU member states are not the only way to organize joint communication initiatives and reaching out to the European public.

Therefore, the Commission believes that establishing strategic partnerships through special projects with regional and local authorities and organizations can play a crucial role in initiating debate on the European Union. This will be instrumental in explaining the local relevance of EU decisions and policies to the European community (Commission of the European, 2007). Another issue that was mentioned on the EU Web site by the Commission was that most of the EU issues are presented from a national perspective via the national mass mediated channels of the EU member states. This means that EU policies that may directly affect the lives of EU citizens are presented from a national perspective under the influence of national interests. This is an important challenge the EU institutions have to deal with. The Commission suggested that the EU institutions need to engage in direct and two-way communication with EU citizens in national, regional, and local contexts.

The Commission suggests that one way of achieving this is through communicating with national and European level political parties to reach out to people directly. Here is a summary of the Commission's efforts to communicate with the EU citizens and residents, including the immigrant community about EU immigrant integration efforts. First of all, the Commission recommends a study/mapping exercise of the various rights and obligations of TCNs in the EU member states (Common programme, 2007). This way, the Commission will be able to create a list of the differences in the treatment and rights of TCNs in different EU member states. I believe that this might be a good strategy for the EU institutions to connect with the various immigrant groups and to listen to their needs and problems, eventually leading to a deeper understanding of the issues TCNs face in various EU member states.

The creation of a platform of immigrant organizations at the EU level is also proposed by the Commission. This platform of immigrant organizations might be very useful for the different immigrant associations to engage in projects and be more instrumental in informing their stakeholders about the EU immigrant integration efforts. Federations and associations established by different immigrant groups could join this platform to voice their opinions about immigrant integration in the European Union. In addition, the Commission recommends that intercultural, inter- and intra-faith dialogue platforms should be created in the EU member states to increase dialogue among religious and civil organizations at the national level. This might also provide an opportunity for immigrant organizations to engage in relationships and partnerships at the national level and expand the national association networks.

The Commission also plans to launch a Web portal for European experiences on immigrant integration which will include a European Integration Forum to encourage EU level participation by all stakeholders (Common programme, 2007). A presence on the Internet might be influential in reaching out to more immigrants and creating an EU-wide network where people could share their experiences and look for answers to their questions about EU immigrant integration efforts. 176 One of the Commission's goals is to increase civil society organizations' access to the Commission by allocating a person as a civil society contact point for all departments (Commission of the European, 2007). A specific contact could also be allocated for the area of immigrant integration to provide a direct access point for immigrant associations. Another project of the Commission is the Houses of Europe to create European public spaces as meeting points for citizens, NGOs, political actors, and the mass media (Commission of the European, 2007).

These spaces could also be used by the immigrant communities to attend and organize special events such as exhibitions, film screenings, meetings, and forums. These spaces may allow immigrant communities and associations to voice their concerns about issues related to immigrant integration and share their experiences. In addition, intercultural projects organized by different immigrant communities could also be held in these spaces. The Commission also proposed to present EU policy initiatives to the general public by policy specialists in Brussels and the EU member states the day they have been adopted (Commission of the European, 2007). This strategy could also be used to raise awareness and boost public debate on EU immigrant integration legislations both at the EU and the national level. As it can be understood from the examination of the EU communication strategies, the Commission, and other EU institutions emphasize the need to communicate with the EU citizens and start a public debate on the future of Europe and other EU policies.

Another goal of the Commission is to establish stronger relationships with member states, NGOs, civil society associations, and opinion leaders in the member states to expand the EU communication structure and reach out to as many stakeholders as possible through various networks and platforms created at the European Union and member state level. 177 However, one also quickly realizes that a targeted communication or public relations strategy specifically designed for immigrants or for enhancing immigrant integration does not currently exist among the EU communication strategies. However, involving the immigrant communities and immigrant associations in the public sphere and establishing relationships with them are proposed in the Commission's Common Agenda for Integration and the Communicating Europe in Partnership documents. These documents can be seen as a starting point where the needs and concerns of specific civil society organizations and immigrant associations are acknowledged.

Involvement with the EU institutions and uniting in EU-wide platforms or networks at the national level may benefit these organizations as they will establish relationships with EU institutions, engage in two-way communication, and influence legislation through expressing their needs and problems. Immigrant associations and communities may also be involved in these strategies and be able to better inform their members on EU immigrant integration decisions and new developments in this area. In addition, the intercultural, inter-, and intra-faith dialogue platforms proposed in the Common Agenda for Integration may also be instrumental in starting a dialogue with religious and civil organizations at the national level. This stress on the civil society organizations and immigrant associations reflects the fact that the European Union has realized the importance of involving these groups in the EU public sphere and providing a platform to voice their opinions.

The "Communicating Europe in Partnership" document, which will be discussed in detail below, contains a brief reference to public diplomacy in the European Union addressing the public of the third countries. The Commission's communication activities in third countries aim to strengthen the image of the EU as a global actor and to build good relationships through pro-active public diplomacy, thereby helping the Commission achieve its external policy goals. This statement reveals that the European Union sees public diplomacy as a strategy to be used in establishing and maintaining relationships with third countries and does not regard its communication with the public of the EU member states as public diplomacy. This information is worth noting. Later, the word communication was also searched and this search revealed important results. I believe that the communication strategies of the European Union are same as public relations strategies, but just named as communication. Below are the results for the search for the word communication.

Directorate General Communication

European Commission Directorate General (DG) Communication was established to inform the EU citizens, the world public, the mass media, and other organizations about the European Union. The objectives of DG Communication are in parallel with the Commission's objectives for the years 2005-2009, which emphasizes that the citizens should be informed about and involved in the challenges facing the European Union, and these efforts should exceed Brussels-based political settings and reach the European public space.

DG Communication stresses the need for interinstitutional coordination through partnerships between the EU institutions and the member states. Thus, four objectives have been put forward, which include developing communication strategies that address the concerns of EU citizens; initiating partnerships between the major players in communication in Europe; creating an EU public sphere and initiating debate on the European Union; and increasing the availability of services in order to improve the Commission's communication quality and abilities.

The communication priorities set by the DG Communication are: The European Parliament elections in 2009; energy and climate change; 20th anniversary of democratic change in Central and Eastern Europe; and sustainable growth, jobs, and solidarity. In addition, the Commission has two of its own communication priorities, which include the issues of future of Europe for citizens and Europe in the world. The DG Communication Web site includes the EU Press Room, a section called SCADplus, which includes summaries of legislation, and General Publications, which can be reached online or requested. The Easy Reading Corner provides access to EU documents. Those interested can also reach EU -based news releases through the Press Release Rapid service on the Web site. Europe Direct, which is an information service for EU citizens, provides a direct contact to the EU via a toll-free phone number, email, or online help to provide information about the EU upon request.

DG Communication announces a large number of public procurement contracts for services, works, and supplies every year, based on demand. These service contracts may be for services needed in headquarters and departments in Brussels or the Commission's representations in the member states. Multimedia Actions, is one of the procurements of the 2009, focusing on the co-production and! or dissemination of audiovisual information to publicize Commission policies and decisions, and their assessment through surveying target groups. Media Information, another procurement for the year 2009, aims to provide the mass media with tools for better understanding and reporting of current affairs. Strategies include increasing and diversifying audiovisual production and dissemination on technological platforms; participating in audiovisual trade shows and festivals open to the general public; and organize seminars and training events for journalists to maximize the coverage of the European Parliament elections[74].

Local Communication Activities procurement concerns the implementation of a decentralized communication strategy via the Commission representations in member states, thus using communication tools tailored to local audiences. These communication activities are to address the communication objectives of DG Communication. Organization of seminars and conferences is also one of the procurements of the DG communication for 2009. These are to interest the general public and bring together parliamentarians, national, regional, and local authorities, Commissioners, mass media professionals, non-profit organizations and opinion leaders to debate EU issues ("Annual work programme," 2008). Some other procurement projects focus on public opinion analysis, operation of the Europe Direct online information and

[74] Woodard, Blair DeWitt. "Intimate Enemies: Visual Culture and U.S.-Cuban Relations, 1945--2000." Order No. 3422400, The University of New Mexico, 2010. In PROQUESTMS ProQuest Dissertations & Theses Full Text, http://search.proquest.com/docview/757372624?accountid=120 85.

communication tools, targeted written publications aimed at the design of local publications produced by the Representations, and written publications of general interest ("Annual work programme," 2008).

In addition to the procurements, DG Communication awards grants to organizations or individuals that provide information about the European Union. The objectives of these EU funded communication projects are to inform EU citizens about the European Union and the main issues facing it. Awards for organizations in different EU member states are distributed by the Commission's representations ("Grants," n.d.).

Public opinion analysis also falls under the functions of DG Communication. Public opinion in the member states is monitored to evaluate public opinion, use in the EU documents, and assist in decision-making. Euro barometer surveys and other studies that focus on EU citizenship, enlargement, social situation, health, culture, information technology, environment, etc., can be reached from the DG Communication Web site ("Public opinion," n.d.). Another component of the DG Communication is Audiovisual Services, which contains videos, audio files, and photos about the European Union. EbS, the European Union's TV information service, provides audiovisual material about the European Union via satellite to media professionals. The programming includes live events, news items, and other audiovisual material on EU policies and issues[75]. In fact, in a section on the Web site called Get Your Facts Straight contains an important statement about the EU's weaknesses in terms of communicating to the public. This weakness is due to the fact that news about the European Union reaches the EU public through national mass media and communication channels of the member states. DG Communication points to this issue and tries to address the false or misleading news stories from its Web site: Most of us rely on our national newspapers, television and radio news to find out about what is going on in the EU.

Unfortunately, amongst the clear and informative reports lie a large number of stories based on twisted facts or even lies. The stories can make entertaining reading, but many people believe them and often come away with a picture of the EU as a bunch of mad 'eurocrats'. These pages take some of those stories and set the record straight - sadly, we cannot keep track of them all.

---

[75] Westrum, Andrew T. "Global Health Diplomacy: A Multi-Method Critical Success Factor Analysis." Order No. 3489120, Central Michigan University, 2011. In PROQUESTMS ProQuest Dissertations & Theses Full Text, http://search.proquest.com/docview/912382119?accountid=120 85.

Communicating Europe in Partnership

The "Communicating Europe in Partnership" document, consolidated by the signature of the European Parliament, the Council and the Commission on Oct. 22, 2008, provides an overview of the Commission's communication strategy and forms the basis for DG Communication's actions and strategies. In this document, the Commission suggests that the debate on Europe needs to involve not just the EU institutions but the citizens. Accordingly, EU communication initiatives must focus on listening, two-way communication through the active participation of citizens and "going local". The main component of this document is to include those involved in the decision-making process in the communication of the EU issues. The Communication lays down the conditions for an EU communication policy on two fronts: A communication policy based on consulting the public and a partnership with political, economic and social players in the member states.

Coherent and Integrated Communication

The objective of building communication partnerships between different EU institutions and member states is to enable EU citizens to understand the impact of EU policies at European, national, and local level. Thus the Commission proposes an inter-institutional framework to improve cooperation on the EU communication process and nurturing exchanges and understanding between EU institutions, the general public, and the civil society. This need is a result of the fact that the EU issues are mostly presented from a national perspective through the mass media of the member states. Consequently, the European Union policies, actions, and issues that affect the lives of EU citizens directly are not presented from a transnational perspective. This is an important challenge for the EU institutions. The Commission intends to improve its communication strategies engaging in two-way communication with EU citizens in national, regional, and local contexts in addition to communicating with national and European level political parties, contributing to the development of a "European public sphere".

Empowering Citizens

The Commission underlines the need for open debate at the EU level enabling citizens to express their opinions on EU issues and policies. The European Union may benefit from the communication resources and experiences of NGOs, associations, and other entities to reach the European public and initiate public debate[76].

---

[76] Veisz, Elizabeth. ""Well-Dispos'd Savages": Elite Masculinity in Eighteenth-Century British Literature." Order No. 3443519, University of Maryland, College Park, 2010. In PROQUESTMS ProQuest Dissertations & Theses Full Text, http://search.proquest.com/docview/854984341?accountid=120 85.

Going local

One way of reaching out to EU citizens is communicating through channels at the regional and local levels. The Commission used a pilot project in representations in the eleven member states where additional communication staff were hired to reach out to more citizens, the mass media and improve public debate on the European Union in their respective countries. The project was successful and the Commission plans to increase the communication staff in additional representations.

Another pilot project was also launched in 2007-2008 to create European public spaces, called the Houses of Europe in Tallinn, Dublin, and Madrid. The goal was to attract the public, create a new image for the European Union, and create a meeting point for citizens, NGOs, political actors, and the mass media. The spaces were to be used for exhibitions, films, meetings, visits, discussions, forums and lectures focusing mainly on civil society, politics, education, academia, think tanks and the cultural world

.

Another strategy proposed by the Commission was to present EU policy initiatives by policy specialists to interested parties and the general public on the day of their adoption, simultaneously in Brussels and in Member States, depending on the resources available to the Representations and policy departments. The commission believes that this will raise awareness and boost public debate on EU legislations at the local level.

Active European citizenship

In this document, the Commission states that the education for active citizenship falls under the responsibility of the EU member states. Peoples' rights and duties as European citizens are taught as part of the school curriculum in less than half of the EU member states and the history of European integration is taught in 20 member states. However, the Commission proposes a Lifelong Learning program, which includes education for active citizenship and promote civic competences through programs organized by civil society organizations. Thus the Commission plans to increase civil society organizations' access to the Commission by naming a specific civil society contact point in each of its departments[77].

---

[77] McEachern, Jaclyn O'Brien. "Diplomatic Activity in Service of Papal Teaching: The Promotion of Religious Freedom in Relations with Selected Islamic States during the Pontificate of John Paul II." Order No. 3427675, The Catholic University of America, 2010. In PROQUESTMS ProQuest Dissertations & Theses Full Text, http://search.proquest.com/docview/815229484?accountid=120 85.

Developing a European Public Sphere

The Commission asserts that there are many political decisions taken at the EU level which affect everyday lives of Europeans. Conversely, this "relevance of the European Union to its citizens" needs to be better communicated to the public. What's more, the EU decisions are usually taken after heated debates. These debates are important and they can only emerge if the proposed issues and policies influence the policies of member states. The Commission suggests that the public also needs to be involved in these debates through not just national, but transnational communication channels. The Commission also proposes that the Commission representations in member states should organize meetings with relevant stakeholders to receive their input on EU policies as part of developing the EU public sphere.

Partnership Approach

The Inter-institutional Group on Information (IGI), chaired jointly by the European Parliament, the Commission, and the Presidency, determines communication strategies and priorities for the EU institutions and member states. The proposed collaboration with the EU member states for enhanced communication is crucial because polling results show that citizens expect their national government to inform them about what the EU is doing for them and how this affects their daily lives.

Member states should be better informed to provide relevant and up-to-date information to their citizens. However, partnerships with EU member states are not the only way to organize joint communication initiatives. Strategic partnerships with regional and local authorities and associations, through special projects, can also play a crucial role in initiating debate on the Europe Union and be instrumental in explaining the local relevance of EU decisions and policies[78].

Communication of Immigrant Integration The European Migration Network (EMN)

The Commission proposed on August 10, 2007 the Council to establish a European Migration Network (EMN) composed of the Commission and the National Contact Points. The goal of EMN is to provide European institutions and member states up-to-date and objective information on migration and asylum, and thus support policy development and decision making. The EMN will also be responsible for collaborating with other European and international bodies; publishing reports on migration and asylum in the European Union; the development and maintenance of an online information system for

[78] Brodsky, Lauren Naomi. "Democracy Across the Airwaves: The Strategic Work of American International Broadcasting in Azerbaijan and Iran." Order No. 3422072, Fletcher School of Law and Diplomacy (Tufts University), 2010. In PROQUESTMS ProQuest Dissertations & Theses Full Text, http://search.proquest.com/docview/755479271?accountid=120 85.

relevant documents and publications; and the preparation of the annual program of activities ("The European migration," 2008).

Mutual information procedure concerning national measures

The Council passed a decision on October 5, 2006, asking for the establishment of a Web- based mutual information network run by the Commission. The goal is to allow the exchange of views on member states' national measures in the areas of asylum and immigration. In addition, the Commission will prepare a report each year summarizing information transmitted by the member states each year, which will be presented to the Parliament and the Council to promote further discussion on national asylum and immigration policies ("Mutual information," 2007).

Community statistics on asylum and migration

The European Parliament and of the Council passed a decision in July 11,2007 for the compilation of statistics on migration and foreign workers. This decision was also an extension of the Commission's 2003 action plan for developing Community statistics on migration. According to this decision, member states are required to provide Eurostat with statistics on the numbers of immigrants who moved to and emigrants who moved from the territory of the member state; current residents; residence permits and long-term residence permits issued; and persons who acquired citizenship[79].

Public Diplomacy in the Information Age

The world is changing fundamentally. Images and information respect neither time nor borders. Hierarchy is giving way to networking, and openness is crowding out secrecy and exclusivity. Ideas and capital move swiftly and unimpeded across a global network of governments, corporations, and nongovernmental organizations. In this world o f instantaneous information and communication, traditional diplomacy is struggling to sustain its relevance. Fundamental forces that demand change in the practice of American diplomacy include: the revolution in information technology, a proliferation of new media, the globalization of business and finance, a widening public participation in international relations, and complex issues that transcend national boundaries.

The major mover of change is information technology. The Internet is expected to reach one billion people by 200S and to be available to half the world's population by 2010. This network will

[79] Lavender, Wayne. "Worldview and Public Policy: From American Exceptionalism to American Empire." Order No. 3399168, George Mason University, 2010. In PROQUESTMS ProQuest Dissertations & Theses Full Text, http://search.proquest.com/docview/219894411?accountid=120 85.

become the backbone of future relations between nation-states, corporations and individuals. The global Internet has connected together people, institutions, and countries more tightly than they have ever been. It has forced, into close connection, individuals and groups that have not always been good neighbours. And it has accelerated the evolution of legal, social, and economic institutions. In this environment, the government is not the only source of information and it has limited power to control the dissemination of information. Information on foreign affairs can be transmitted by any number of private individuals, companies, community organizations, and on-line chat rooms.

In an editorial entitled, "Foreign Policy 3.1," New York Times columnist Thomas L. Friedman posited that transnational corporations, such as Microsoft, have an influence on foreign policy. "U.S. foreign policy will be shaped to a significant degree by decisions taken in Washington—Redmond, Washington," Friedman proclaimed. Few would dispute that technology has changed the environment in which diplomacy takes place. Two complementary technologies account for the changes the world is witnessing today: computers and telecommunications.

Today's personal computers, selling for a couple hundred dollars, operate ten times faster than a 1970 IBM mainframe computer that sold for nearly SS million.101 By 2010, prices are expected to have plunged to less than $100. The cost of telecommunications has not dropped as dramatically, but the decline is accelerating due to fibre-optic cables, satellites, digitization, and deregulation. When these two technologic—computers and telecommunications-are integrated into networks of connectivity, opportunities for new applications will proliferate. Information technology is changing our lives, our society, our institutions, our culture. Yet there remain many constants, including time and human relations. Traditionalists who insist that diplomacy need not change are wrong, but so are those who insist that it must change completely.

Finding a balance that honours the past and respects the future is the challenge facing America's diplomatic corps. Contemporary diplomatic practices were honed in an era when the American press was perceived as a means to amplify the government's version of international news. Edward R. Munow's reports from London during World War II supported the American conduct o f the war. That all changed three decades later, when Walter Cronkite's reports suggested that American policy in Vietnam was wrong-headed. People came to the realization that the government and the media have two contradictory versions of the truth, and trust in both institutions declined as a result.

Demand for larger shares of the viewing audience has driven television news networks to reduce their international coverage in the past two decades. Some commentators assume that the media are making American foreign policy, and policymakers have felt their impact. Former Secretary to State Madeleine Albright told the Senate Foreign Relations Committee, "Television's ability to bring graphic images of pain and outrage into our living rooms has heightened the pressure both for immediate engagement in areas of international crisis and immediate disengagement when events do not go according to plan." However, the "CNN effect" is less powerful than many previously assumed. While the media can be a force in decision-making, their role is minimal when policy is clearly formed, articulated, and supported.

Former Washington time's correspondent Warren Strobel, argued in Late-Breaking Foreign Policy that the media take their cue from the executive, Congress, and relief organizations.103 Recent research also has shown that the "CNN effect" has been overstated. Policy-makers should consider the media, but they should not be subservient to their role. The media are not heady instruments of foreign policy, but rather interactive elements in a complex process. Where the global market influences editorial decisions, it is fair to say that globalization will lead to a greater concentration of media ownership. However, the price of entering the publishing or broadcasting sectors is dramatically lower than it ever has been.

With moderate technological know-how, a personal computer and modem, almost anyone can be a self-publisher and have an Internet presence. While a handful of corporations will control the major media markets, alternative media outlets will continue to proliferate. Merrill Brown, editor-in-chief of MSNBC Online, predicted that Web sites that provide audio and video on demand will become tomorrow's primary source of news and information. He said several million people use the Internet as their daily news source, and MSNBC Online already averages 350,000 users per day[80].

According to the Pew Research Centre, the number o f Americans obtaining their news on the Internet is growing at an astonishing rate. A 1998 news consumption survey found that 36 million Americans are reading news on the Internet at least once a week.105 By March 2001, the number of Americans reading news online had jumped to 64 million.106 The time that it takes a rumour or speculation started in one place to find its way into local radio and television broadcasts can now be measured in minutes, rather than days or weeks. As Internet access becomes more readily available, the important criteria for choice will be technical excellence, content, and trust. Consumers will turn to news sources they can trust. The public will become more fragmented and specialized, such that governments will find it more difficult to develop a national consensus on public policy.

---

[80] Gagnon, Michelle Leona. "Global Health Diplomacy: Understanding how and Why Health is Integrated into Foreign Policy." Order No. NR98101, University of Ottawa (Canada), 2012. In PROQUESTMS ProQuest Dissertations & Theses Full Text, http://search.proquest.com/docview/1356851849?accountid=12085.

On the other hand, authoritarian governments will also find it more difficult to manipulate publics. As the Internet grows and direct broadcast satellites proliferate, governments will have more channels than ever to communicate their message; this proliferation of channels could see a resurgence of international news coverage. Globalization of finance and business has diminished the relevance of national boundaries. The constraints of distance are disappearing in the information economy. Markets are becoming more efficient, but also more volatile. As communities, governments, organizations and individuals that have never been neighbours are brought together, profound forces collide, and it could take years, or decades, before new invisible and intangible boundaries are established. While some argue that most nations will benefit from globalization, others fear growing disparities between the rich and the poor.108 While there are many differences between this and the previous century, the greatest is the role of information in the global economy.

The primary source of wealth in the United States has been transformed from manufacturing industries to the service sector, and the knowledge worker is the key to continuing American prosperity. Because o f the new technologies and liberalized trade regimes, there has been a resurgence o f trade and migration, an explosion in capital flows, and an unprecedented exchange o f information among countries. Peter Schwartz and Peter Leyden wrote, "We are watching the beginnings of a global economic boom on a scale never experienced before."109 They believe that the global economy, driven by advances in information technology, will continue its surge for at least another two decades. The road ahead will not be without bumps, even some major detours.

Globalization contributes to new economic problems. One example is the East Asian currency meltdown, which began in Thailand in mid-1997. The depreciation of the Thai baht led to dire warnings by the U.S. Federal Reserve and the expression of security concerns by the White House. In this environment, a Centre for Strategic and International Studies report upheld that diplomacy plays a critical stabilizing role. "When other nations deny market access or compete unfairly, diplomacy must ensure that the international agreements are honoured. And when financial instability threatens, the U.S. must take the lead to restore order." The public dimension o f the digital age receives less attention, but it may be the most significant change to the conduct of diplomacy. Virtually no major foreign affairs or domestic initiative is taken today without first testing public opinion.

Individual citizens are developing new competencies for global activism, such that this public dimension is fast becoming the central element of the new diplomacy. It is a common perception that Americans have lost interest in foreign affairs. Yet, despite the perception of an uninvolved public, polling data from the past several years demonstrate that public opinion is very fluid, sometimes leading, sometimes lagging behind elite opinion. Elites tend to underestimate the public's support for American engagement abroad, exaggerating the differences that separate them and confusing ignorance for apathy. Yet, there appears to be a public willingness to respond positively to U.S. leadership on international issues. A 1994 study by the Chicago Council on Foreign Relations compared "leader" and public opinions on foreign policy issues.

It found that public attitudes had remained remarkably stable, but foreign policy concerns were noticeably absent from the public's "top-ten list" of problems facing the country. However, the public did demonstrate an elevated interest in foreign policy concerns that related to local issues: stopping the flow of illegal drugs, protecting American jobs in a global economy, and reducing illegal immigration. A 1999 study found that 61 percent of the public support an active role for the United States in the world, and 96 percent of leaders favour such activism. Fifty percent of the public believe America plays a more important and powerful role as a world leader today than 10 years ago, and more than three-quarters of the public (79 percent) and 71 percent of leaders foresee the United States playing an even greater role 10 years from now.

Public opinion does not exist in a vacuum, but is developed and nurtured by opinion leaders in the government and press. If Congress and the administration do not lead, it should not be expected that leadership on international issues will emerge from the public. If there is any surprise, it is that public opinion has remained so stable in the absence of a coherent vision of the U.S. role in the world.

Within this landscape, the one critical element that binds government and the public is trust. In a world that is vulnerable to "information overload," information alone is a useless commodity. Reliable, trusted interpreters are needed, but where can one turn for reliable information on international relations? From the time of the Vietnam build-up through the election o f Ronald Reagan, trust in the federal government has plummeted. For diplomacy to be effective, it must be backed by a public willing to trust government to act wisely on its behalf. Absent that mist, people will turn to other institutions that have earned their trust. The information age poses intense challenges to public diplomacy, either magnifying international disagreement and discord, or distracting people from vital concerns abroad.

At a time when international commerce was largely conducted between nations and when communication was relatively slow, the traditional tools of diplomacy were appropriate and adequate. However, with instantaneous communication and capital movement, and with the addition of numerous new actors, classic diplomacy no longer suffices.

Neither yesterday's diplomatic culture nor its technology will survive in this complex environment. New diplomatic tools and training will be required to weather the storms of change and to ensure global stability. Several assailant features of this new environment merit comment. The first is connectivity. Small changes have distant and unpredictable consequences. The second characteristic of the new environment is speed.

Decision-making must be accelerated if it is to be effective. Modem technology and efficient practices must be adopted to ensure that government is a real-time actor in rapidly unfolding international events. The third is the proliferation of new actors. This is the public dimension of the digital age. Power is broadly shared by government with businesses, NGOs, universities, and interested publics—and amplified by the media. The fourth is the feedback from the environment, which requires a rich flow of relevant and accurate information and a system that operates on public trust. In this complex environment, control is elusive.

Recent research has pointed to a waning interest in international relations in the United States as the general public turns its focus inward to address more pressing domestic concerns. Intense competition for an increasingly fragmented market audience will encourage media to sensationalize international conflicts and thus, erode the opportunities for informed dialogue. International financial and economic interdependence could become a destabilizing force, converting local problems into global nightmares. And, as a CSIS report noted, the trend towards a convergence o f information and entertainment will persist and Walter Lippmann's distinction between "the world outside and the pictures in our heads" will become blurred as images multiply exponentially. The third Summit of the Americas, which convened in Canada April 20, 2001, recognized the new prominence connectivity has come to occupy as a national and hemispheric goal of sovereign nations and international organizations.

A background document prepared for the Organization of American States Special Committee on Inter- American Summits Management observed the need to develop hemispheric "connectivity for community" in the information age. It recognized that the world is undergoing dramatic transformation by information and communications technologies (ICTs) and the rapid pace o f innovation and change. The information revolution is stimulating fundamental changes in democratic, economic and social institutions: New technologies are breaking down barriers, expanding dialogues and altering the nature o f the relationships between government, the private sector, and civil society.

The OAS background paper perceived connectivity, not as the solution to all human problems, but as a tool for human development. "Support for a connectivity agenda does not imply the abandonment of more fundamental development objectives. . . . A comprehensive commitment to development can and should encompass not only efforts to meet basic needs, but to ensure that the benefits of new and emerging technologies are more broadly shared and that opportunities to participate in knowledge- based economies are expanded." The OAS believes that the development and distribution o f information technology and connectivity holds the promise of "unprecedented opportunities for political, economic and social development in the Americas"" The OAS Special Committee on Inter-American Summits Management said the challenge to closer hemispheric integration is to ensure that the potential benefits of connectivity are maximized and shared by the greatest number of people and by closing digital divides within and between countries.

The third Summit of the Americas was to consider how information and communications technology could assist participant nations in advancing a common agenda o f strengthening democracy, creating prosperity, and realizing human potential. The body proposed initiatives that would promote more equitable access to and distribution o f the benefits of technology "in the interest of enhancing prosperity, reducing insecurity and strengthening the hemispheric community. . . "" 8 The principal objective of improving connectivity in the Americas was to create new instruments and linkages to "sustain diversity, enhance understanding, extend the ability o f governments to provide services, empower citizens to improve their lives, and bring new knowledge and skills to those who need them." In the digital age, the United States must take advantage of the benefits of connectivity to promote acceptance of American values and policies abroad through public diplomacy.

Challenges to Public Diplomacy

One challenge diplomacy faces in the future is to keep the American public informed o f and engaged in international affairs. President Harry S. Truman said the foreign policy of the United States rests upon the support of the public. He believed the American public is neither naive nor innocent. When based upon whatever degree o f information has been handed to them, Truman insisted that people manage to accumulate enough knowledge to understand the issues o f the day. Former Ambassador Philip Habib believed the problem is not the ignorance of the general public, but rather, the incompetence of the officials who represent them. "The capacity of the American people to deal with these issues is much greater than intellectuals are likely to give them credit for. Their confidence that they understand what they are being told and have the ability to react to it, is shaken by only one thing—their lack of confidence in elected and appointed officials"[81].

---

[81] Harris, Richard J. "Ambassador Doraemon: Japan's Pop Culture Diplomacy in China and South Korea." Order No. 1508566, Georgetown University, 2012. In PROQUESTMS ProQuest Dissertations & Theses Full Text, http://search.proquest.com/docview/1010625651?accountid=12 085.

American Foreign Service Association President F. A. 'Tex" Harris said at a 1994 USIA symposium that he believes the key to securing the engagement of the American public in U.S. foreign policy resides in effective presidential leadership. "Can we engage the public through presidential leadership so that there is an understanding that American policies and American presence abroad are in fact related to American jobs and the quality of life here in the United States?" Harris asked. Former USIA Association President David Gergen agreed that the single most important question in American foreign policy today is how to convince the public to remain engaged. He suggested that the answer lies in domestic reform and renewal. "If this country is to deteriorate inside, and we turn toward greater class antagonism, racial antagonism, ethnic antagonism, then I will tell you, we will withdraw from the world.

That's when we are going to turn more paranoid, we are going to turn xenophobic, and our foreign policy is going to be extremely difficult to sustain on an international basis. To me, that's fundamental. Domestic reform is terribly important to the success o f our foreign policy, to be able to sustain public support for foreign policy. Beyond that, I think we have to engage the country on levels that have been different from the past." Although one may disagree with Gergen's call for domestic renewal, bolstering public support for U.S. foreign policies is critical to the future success of diplomacy. The United States must exert leadership in the international arena. No longer under the exigencies of the Cold War, the United States owns special responsibilities and opportunities as the sole remaining superpower to address an expanded roster o f global issues and concerns.

America does not have the power to force change in the world by itself, nor can it solve the world's problems alone. However, it is equally apparent that the world's great problems won't be solved without American leadership. People will look to the United States for leadership, but they will also demand that they be treated with respect and dignity. In this context, if America hopes to influence the policies of its friends and allies overseas, it must bolster old alliances and initiate new partnerships. Public opinion and understanding in foreign countries are as vital to the success of American foreign policy as they are to building domestic support for policies at home. As America pursues its foreign policy objectives through aggressive public diplomacy campaigns, it must not neglect the power of personal relationships. Partnerships are formed and maintained through skilful relationship building.

The U.S. government must have people on the ground in foreign countries who understand what America is all about and who are able to transmit that message to foreign publics. The mission of U.S. public diplomacy is to tell America's story in a way that touches the hearts and minds of people of other countries. As advertising guru Steve Hayden124 asserted, u[T]o communicate with clarity and power, and maybe to change the world a little for the better, you must touch people emotionally as well as rationally." At the 2001 Net Diplomacy Conference, Hayden pointed out that America has excellent "brand" values. A brand "is the intangible sum of a product's attributes: its name, packaging and price, its history, and the way it's advertised.

A brand is also defined by consumers' impressions of the people who use it, as well as their own experience." A brand is not a product, but a relationship. Products are tangible and can be experienced through the senses, whereas brands are intangible. They are about trust and feeling and emotional connection. People project their hopes, dreams and sometimes their fears on brands. In like manner, American diplomats are the stewards and caretakers of the largest brand of all: the American dream. The United States is not die only country thinking about its brand identity. England has a government-sponsored "Brand England" program. Belgium followed an image repair and development program after a series o f "incidents" damaged the country's reputation. France held a nationwide contest to find a woman to represent the Spirit of Liberty - "La Liberte" - whose visage now adorns every public office and every government Web site. India hired a public relations firm to produce a global brand analysis to help it identify which unique characteristics the country could leverage to pursue its national interests.

In an environment where public participation in international affairs has grown due to the democratization of information and communication, no foreign policy can succeed without a sustained public diplomacy effort to understand, inform, and influence private individuals and organizations, as well as governments. The digital age brings with it some important changes to the conduct of diplomacy, yet some elements are timeless. Former Secretary of State George P. Shultz summarized the aspects that remain the same and identified key changes to the practice of diplomacy in a speech he gave at the U.S. Institute of Peace. First, he said, the diplomat must truly represent the United States. Shultz understood diplomacy as "a fundamental human activity, conducted between people as well as among nations." Second, Shultz believed that a diplomat must be able to speak with authority for his or her country; otherwise, no one will take him or her seriously. Therefore, the good diplomat must build and nurture his or her base of authority.

Third, a diplomat must verify that the other party speaks with his or her government's authority, so that true agreements can be reached. A fourth point relates to the nature of negotiations: international relationships and alliances must offer the possibility of benefit to all parties involved. Former U.S. Ambassador to Turkey William Macomber remarked, the consummate art of the diplomat is to negotiate an agreement that is not only to the advantage of his side, but which contains sufficient advantage to the other side that the latter will wish to keep it. Negotiations are not exercises in charity. Their purpose is to produce results that are advantageous to both sides and produce results that last. Shultz reminded his audience that most negotiations are not one-time events but a process, and that process has its ups and downs. Therefore, the relationship should be constructed with long-term considerations in mind and not on the basis of what is expedient. Sixth, good diplomacy relies on accurate, timely and relevant information.

Writing careful dispatches back home has always been a key function of the U.S. Foreign Service. Reporting has to be solid and well-considered; it has to emerge from deep experience and understanding of the society reported on; and above all, it must be completely accurate.130 Macomber also noted that diplomatic reporting requires accuracy and discrimination. Discriminate reporting is especially important at a time when the sheer volume of diplomatic cable threatens to overwhelm foreign offices and State headquarters. Diplomats must be able to sort through a myriad of facts and determine which is of direct and significant interest to their government's interests.

CNN reporting is no substitute for diplomatic reporting, Shultz said. True, CNN may do it faster and better, but it may not always be accurate. Furthermore, television journalism is not universal. "[Journalism] focuses on places and topics the editors think the viewers are interested in," not on the issues that affect America's national interests. One must distinguish between excellent means o f communication, i.e., the wonders o f information technology, and excellent communication. The bane of the information age is that it makes a mind-boggling flood of information available and making sense o f it all becomes more challenging. This is where Foreign Service Officers in the field prove invaluable; they provide insight, meaning and context to the raw data. Seventh, Shultz said skilful diplomacy is busy at work even in the absence of acute problems and burning crises. Diplomats work to resolve minor disturbances before they become glaring problems. This requires building confidence and understanding, so that when a crisis does arise, one has a solid base from which to work. Vision and strategic ideas are essential[82].

Without a strategic plan and vision, one can very easily lose way as he tries to cope with the constant barrage of "mini-crises" that inevitably spring up. Finally, Shultz said, there is die essential interplay between strength and diplomacy to consider. The two go hand-in-hand. Diplomacy without strength—military and economic—is fruitless, but strength without diplomacy is unsustainable. In marrying diplomacy to power, Shultz rendered a realist interpretation of the relations between nation-states, similar to Hans J.

---

[82] Buddenhagen, Caroline Riker. "Fine Line Or Hard Line? the Tension between Security and Public Diplomacy in Visa Policy before and After 9/11." Order No. 1556256, Georgetown University, 2013. In PROQUESTMS ProQuest Dissertations & Theses Full Text, http://search.proquest.com/docview/1540813427?accountid=12 085.

Morgenthau's definition of diplomacy. "Diplomacy, however morally unattractive its business may seem to many," Morgenthau wrote, "is nothing but a symptom of the struggle for power among sovereign nations, which try to maintain orderly and peaceful relations among themselves."

Ambassador Marc Grossman, President George W. Bush's Under Secretary of State for Political Affairs, would concur with Shultz' assessment that diplomats in the 21st century must command more skills than their predecessors. Grossman told an audience of public diplomacy officials that 21st century diplomats must be proficient not only in languages, but also in inter-cultural communication. They must be effective managers, knowing how to get the most from their people and how to develop each of their subordinates to their fullest potential. Twenty-first century diplomats must possess a broad understanding o f global issues. They must understand the important role that public diplomacy plays in America's relations with both established and emerging democracies around the world.

Twenty-first century diplomats must possess negotiating skills. They must also be able to deal effectively with nongovernmental organizations, the media, and the private sector. They must understand the principles of preventive diplomacy and international peace operations, and they must be comfortable with the latest technologies, which are constantly changing and will continue to change in ways we cannot imagine today. The raw material of diplomacy is information—getting it, assessing it, putting it into the system for the benefit or puzzlement of others. The world is also much more open than ever before. Even authoritarian, closed societies have a hard time keeping important developments to themselves, or keeping their own citizens from knowing what is goes on inside, let alone outside, their borders. And any society that aspires to be a part o f the modem world simply cannot operate in a closed, compartmentalized system. Sovereignty is still a clear and powerful concept, but its meaning has been altered.

The media will play a larger role in this environment; with their elevated role, media must assume greater responsibilities than ever before. This interplay between events and the media produces a phenomenon some have called "quantum diplomacy." "An axiom of quantum diplomacy is that when you observe and measure some piece o f the system, you inevitably disturb the whole system. So the process of observation is itself a cause of change." The struggle to speak with authority for one's country will become more difficult the secretary of State must struggle, not only with colleagues in the executive branch and with member's o f Congress, but also with groups that hold widely diverse, sometimes conflicting, agendas.

The Internet has a democraticizing influence on society, in that it brings more people into the mix and gives them tools to amplify their opinions and multiply the impact of their actions. That is not to say that the trend toward decentralization in modem organizations grants people leave to "do their own thing," nor does it imply that headquarters or command centres no longer matter in die digital age. Nonetheless, information technology is producing a radical shakedown of strictly hierarchical organizations and societies. It is redefining the centre in ways that are more inclusive and which allow governments to be more responsive to the needs of their citizens. Once the trend towards decentralization hits the State Department, several management changes will follow. Hiring will be done on a different basis, because the department will look for people who not only can carry out orders from the top, but who can also see the big picture and be a leader and manager for their team.

Furthermore, the State Department will have to bring people into the analytical and decision-making process earlier, before information becomes outdated and irrelevant to policy considerations. In other words, quicker response time and quicker decision-making processes will be required in the new information-rich environment.136 The digital age should enhance accountability in American diplomacy. What one says and does will be recorded in an ever-larger public domain. The quality of one's decisions and one's capacity to execute them effectively will be on display. This spotlight should result in improved performance and accountability. With instantaneous communication, the pressure mounts for rapid reactions and real time operations.

Limitations of the study and suggestions for future study

The first limitation of the study is that it used only 24 country cases for analysis (N=24) due to the limited availability of secondary data. Such a small number of cases did not only yield insufficient statistical power but also restricted the use of SEM analysis by producing negative variances and inadmissible parameter solutions. Therefore, it was not possible to test overall model fit which was originally proposed. And also, less rigorous significance test with the .10 level was conducted here due to relatively a very small size of cases. If more country cases are added from other secondary datasets or additional data gathering methods (e.g., a survey), SEM analysis of an overall model will be feasible, and the results may be more accurate and meaningful. During the analysis, it also became apparent that the FARA dataset has critical limitations. First, not all contracts reported price. Because many contract prices are missing, the sum of PR contract prices does not represent the actual financial resources devoted to international PR efforts.

For example, among the four PR contracts reported for Afghanistan, three contract prices were missing (one reported amount of a $30,000) thereby underestimating Afghanistan's PR efforts. Second, the report reflects only contracts that are active at the time of data collection, and these contracts have different terms. Third, the majority of the countries (19 out of 24) included in the dataset had less than six government driven PR contracts, and thus, the number of PR contracts were extremely skewed to 0 to 5. With such skewed distribution of data, a small number of country cases standing high in PR contract numbers may dominate the statistic result in their favour.

To overcome the limitations of the FARA dataset, new indicators need to be developed to more accurately assess international PR efforts. Two quantified indicators in this study could not capture the variety of PR efforts. One possible indicator is the number of foreign consular offices and their staffing strength. In the news articles analyzed in this study, most readers' opinions or responses to events and developments were provided by staff members working in foreign embassies and consulates in the U.S. who support the interests of their countries by giving feedback to the news media. They also contribute to improving their respective national images by representing the point of view of their own countries and by justifying their perspectives. In addition, other strategic activities programmed by foreign governments (e.g., government-sponsored scholarships for foreign students, student exchange programs, and second language learning programs) are also potential indicators that may explain the influence of international PR. Third, in the model suggested in this study, news coverage mediated the relationship between international PR efforts and public perception.

The results showed a significant relationship between newspaper coverage and public perception rather than between international PR efforts and public perception, which bolsters traditional agenda-setting effects. However, to account for the diverse media environment, other types of media channels should be counted as influential communication sources for foreign publics, such as films, entertainment TV programs, and web sites. Fourth, the results indicate that government-driven PR activities have a limited effect on public perception. People may be influenced mostly by individual-level experience, such as interpersonal relationships with foreign individuals and exposure to foreign cultures through travelling and cultural exchanges, rather than by programmed PR activities from foreign governments. Thus, it may be interesting to compare and contrast the effects of government-driven PR activities and individual-level experiences in future studies.

Lastly, including reverse directional effects (linkage from public perception to media content and international PR efforts, and from news content to international PR efforts) in the analysis may strengthen the model proposed in this study. For example, governments which are concerning about a negative national image among publics in a target country, may deliberately increase the PR efforts to improve their negative images. International PR activities of Iraq government in the U.S. (e.g., PR contracts reported in FARA) are an implicit evidence to show the possibility of reverse directional effect. Although considering reciprocal relationships requires researchers to confront difficulties in time control, these bidirectional interactions may help better understand the relationships among the variables examined in this study.

Implications of the Research for EU Public Relations and Public Diplomacy and Immigrant Integration

This study examined whether the European Union tailors its communication efforts and cooperates with various EU publics, specifically focusing on Turkish immigrant associations in Brussels. I set out with several research questions. Does the European Union have any strategies to engage in a two-way relationship or dialogue with special interest or civil rights groups when developing and communicating a new policy? More specifically, how does the European Union communicate its immigrant integration decisions and initiatives to the EU public and to the immigrant communities? Can immigrant associations have any influence in the EU immigrant integration initiatives and is lobbying or other type of persuasive strategies by immigrant groups possible in the European Union? The research results revealed that the current communication efforts of the European Union are not reaching the Turkish immigrant community. Even the community leaders' lack of knowledge about the EU immigrant integration efforts show that more communication is needed. The EU institutions need to use public relations and public diplomacy strategies to promote EU founding principles and other decisions and initiatives, including issues of immigrant integration to EU internal and external publics.

Managing a relationship with different people who come from different national and cultural backgrounds is the challenge the European Union faces today. However, as Valentini (2007) stressed, supranational organizations such as the European Union "need to communicate with the language, the values and norms of their publics" if they want to reach them and incur behavioural changes in their publics (p. 123). This research also revealed that the European Union needs to utilize public relations and public diplomacy strategies to nurture relationships between publics and the EU institutions and also among the different communities living within the EU borders to enhance community building. Ledingham (2001) proposed that public relations efforts may be influential for community building through nurturing relationships and uniting diverse populations by reducing conflict and resolving differences.

Community building is an important function of public relations that public diplomacy could take lessons from. Utilizing public relations and public diplomacy to integrate its increasingly diverse population and to create a common European identity and enhance community building, especially among the immigrant communities, should be a major goal for the European Union. According to a European Commission report published in November 2007, the population of TCNs within the European Union is 18.5 million, making up 3.8% of the total EU population of approximately 493 million. The 3.8% may seem insignificant; however, 18.5 million TCNs living within EU borders make up a population larger than many EU member states and constitute a large immigrant community. The EU institutions need to acknowledge the significance of the TCN population in Europe and start to overtly consider these immigrant communities in their public relations and public diplomacy efforts as a unique public that need to be communicated with. A new way to ensure enhanced communication with various EU publics, including TCNs, is to engage in dialogue with civil society groups.

Michalski (2007) suggested that this can be done by establishing networks and engaging in two-way communication with interest groups, such as citizens' or civil rights organizations. Interacting with interest groups may be helpful for the EU institutions, especially during the planning or implementation of new decisions or policies. This way, the EU institutions could get the public's input on new policy areas and they can reach publics more effectively about new policies and actions during their implementation. Enhancing communication with diverse publics and engaging in two-way communication are public relations strategies that public diplomacy could use to reach people more

effectively. Some may argue that people do not need
to be informed about EU decisions as these decisions
are not directly relevant to EU publics because laws
and regulations are always implemented at the
national level due to the structure of the European
Union. However, as a researcher conducting research
about communication, I believe that although EU
decisions and initiatives may not influence the lives
of EU publics directly, people still need to be
informed about the European Union.

I believe that this will help enhance the EU
public sphere and also reveal the importance of EU
institutions for the EU citizens and residents. Unless
people know what the EU is trying to achieve and its
goals, they will never be able to fully appreciate its
importance or value for their lives. Today, the EU
institutions need to incorporate public relations
strategies and establish two-way communication
with diverse EU publics. As Valentini (2007) also
suggested, public relationship management within
the European Union should be "culturally oriented
and based on a two-way symmetrical flow of
communication and on community-building
relationships" (p. 127). However, this research
revealed a lack of direct communication between the
EU institutions and the Turkish community.
Considering that the Turkish community constitutes
a great percentage of the immigrant population
within the European Union, the lack of direct
communication with this community living in the EU
capital may imply a lack of relationship management

in the EU institutions towards the immigrant
communities living within the EU borders.

This situation needs to change if the
European Union aims to create a truly diverse EU
public sphere by being inclusive towards all the
groups that live within EU borders. One way for the
EU institutions to enhance relationships with the
immigrant communities, especially the Turkish
immigrant community, is to start to publish EU
documents and reports in Turkish. This way, the
language barrier will be eliminated and the Turkish
immigrant community, the largest in Europe, will be
able to reach and understand EU related information.
I believe that a diverse EU public sphere which takes
into account the views and needs of all EU publics is
possible. But it is only possible with more targeted
and advanced public relations and public diplomacy
efforts. Although public relations belong to the field
of communications and public diplomacy belongs to
the international relations field, both practices have
quite similar goals.

Melissen (2007) said that "a lesson that
public diplomacy can take on board from the
sometimes misunderstood field of PR [public
relations] is that the strength of firm relationships
largely determines the receipt and success of
individual messages and overall attitudes" (p. 21).
The importance of cultivating and establishing
relationships and engaging in two-way
communication with diverse publics are important
areas where public diplomacy could learn from the

strategies and practices of public relations. If public diplomacy, instead focusing on information dissemination, could also focus on building and managing relationships, then a much better relationship could be established between the EU institutions and the EU publics and even the rising Euroskepticism among the EU publics could possibly be reduced. This research reveals that although the fields of public relations and public diplomacy belong to different schools, they are quite similar in nature.

If public diplomacy could benefit from the two-way communication and relationship management focus of the public relations field, then publics could be reached more effectively, their concerns and needs could be taken into account, and community building could be enhanced. The European Union, with its unique structure, its goals of enhancing the EU public sphere and reducing Euroskepticism, could be a testing ground for this new public relations approach to public diplomacy. However, I believe that these public relations and public diplomacy strategies for enhanced communication and establishing relationships should not limited to the efforts of the EU institutions. The EU civil society and immigrant communities should establish themselves as a legitimate force to influence the EU institutions. Empowerment of the EU civil society and the immigrant communities is also very important to influence public policies.

From a civil society perspective, the immigrant community in Europe needs to be more proactive and make use of the new communication technologies to shape EU policies and actions. In fact, the civil society groups in the European Union could be empowered and utilize strategic communication practices more effectively. These civil society groups, specifically the immigrant communities, need to be proactive and communicate back to the EU institutions their concerns and needs. Immigrant communities need to realize their potential for influencing and potentially shaping EU immigrant integration decisions and initiatives, as these may directly influence them. Using public relations and strategic communication to establish a dialogue with the EU institutions could also help immigrant communities to improve their conditions in their host countries and even the reputations of their homelands.

Another strategy immigrant communities could use is to unite and establish a platform to voice their opinions and be more influential in promoting public debate about immigrant integration issues in the European Union. Also, an EU civil society network for immigrant associations can be established to increase interaction among different immigrant associations. This immigrant community network could use public relations and public diplomacy strategies, just like an organization or lobby group, to influence policies, especially EU decisions and initiatives related to immigrant integration. This immigrant community network could help the immigrant communities in the European Union to be accepted as a legitimate group that has a specific mission. This could be a new area to use public relations in the European Union. Public relations research needs to focus more on how the civil society can be empowered to shape policies and decisions in the future. This proposed immigrant community network has many implications for the empowerment of the various immigrant communities living within the European Union.

This network can function as a grassroots movement to empower these communities, help them organize and raise their voices to explain their needs. This kind of self-structured organization can also enhance community building as these different immigrant communities will unite to determine common concerns, share their opinions and requests. Such a network may even be influential in providing information about the immigrant community, in terms of the challenges they face and their needs, back to the EU institutions. The immigrant communities in the European Union need to realize their potential and use communication and public relations strategies to connect their own communities and to establish relationships with the EU institutions. However, the EU institutions also need to improve their public relations, public diplomacy and communication strategies. EU institutions can reach out to immigrant communities more effectively especially if they publish reports or other documents that are related to immigrant integration issues in the native languages of the immigrant communities, for example publish reports in Turkish to reach out to Turkish immigrant associations.

Another recommendation for the EU institutions could be to organize meetings and seminars where the immigrant community leaders could be invited to raise their concerns and to talk about their needs. This way, a personal relationship with the immigrant community leaders and EU officials could be established. These meetings or seminars would also allow the immigrant community leaders to improve their relationships with EU officials and get them inside the doors of the European Union. These meetings or seminars could be provided as Webcasts to those who cannot attend due to geographical limitations. Another recommendation of this research for the European Union is to encourage the contact points in each member state to be more active and to reach out to immigrant communities by attending special events and by personally meeting the immigrant community leaders. This would encourage more interaction between the EU officials and immigrant communities and would help information from these communities to reach EU institutions more effectively.

Another policy or communication strategy I could recommend to the European Union based on secondary research is the need to publicize its initiatives or decisions more effectively if they want to inform EU publics, more specifically the immigrant communities, about what the European Union does and what are its goals. Michalski (2007) also suggested that establishing networks and engaging in two-way communication with interest groups, such as citizens' or civil rights groups, is important, especially if they will influenced by a new decision. Interacting with civil society groups, especially immigrant communities, may be helpful for the European Union while developing new policies and also trying to inform the public about these during their implementation. I believe that if the public could be informed about where certain decisions come from, they may be more inclined to follow the agenda of the European Union and they may be more involved with the EU institutions.

This research has many theoretical implications for the fields of public relations and public diplomacy. First of all, the importance of public relations for large supranational or international organizations has been laid out by this research. Just like countries, these organizations need to utilize public relations and public diplomacy strategies if they want to reach out to their publics, inform them, and to establish relationships with them. As Gilboa (2008) stated, until now the public diplomacy efforts of NGOs, civil society groups, and individuals have mostly been ignored. One point this research underlines is that public relations and public diplomacy are no more unique to corporations or governments anymore. In fact, international organizations need to make use of these strategies to improve their reputations and enhance relationships with their publics. Another point this research makes evident is that the discipline of public diplomacy can feed from the discipline of public relations.

Although these two practices belong to different academic areas, their practices share a lot of common characteristics. As Melissen (2007) argued, the skills and practices of public relations may be used to improve public diplomacy strategies. A major implication of this research is the need for more interaction and research partnerships between the fields of public relations and public diplomacy. Researchers from these fields should collaborate and conduct research together to reveal the similarities between these two fields. Such future studies would be useful for both public relations and public diplomacy as they would increase the application and research areas of both fields.

Recommendations and the EU's Response

These identified challenges to the success of EU public diplomacy have elicited obvious recommendations, which may be summarized as calls for greater unification of EU voice and action, as well as more efforts toward presenting itself as a smart power. The EU has been well aware of critiques and recommendations and has taken steps to implement them. Scholars contend that EU member states are far better off, in terms of public diplomacy and all other aspects, together than they are separately, and so must unite and integrate their separate public diplomacy initiatives.109 States, while they may have robust public diplomacy mechanisms already in place, can only benefit from a combined effort.

As it has been noted, the EU has a positive image in the world as a result of its members, and so member states need not be afraid of losing their clout; they will only gain by having a higher profile as recognized members of the EU. Smaller members who have a low or no global profile will benefit from the collective image even more. As Fiske de Gouviea points out, in this post-Cold War world, collective public diplomacy will not weaken member states' public diplomacy, but will instead limit the criticism of individual states' initiatives as foreign propaganda.110 He argues for centralization of public diplomacy efforts.

Specific recommendations from Fiske de Gouviea's report include creating an EU Public Diplomacy Strategy Committee to centrally review and co-ordinate strategy; creating a database of all EU public diplomacy and external communications activity; increasing polling, surveying, and media monitoring of how the EU is perceived in non-EU rest on the EU's collective military capabilities, the calls for change in this respect are based on prescribed policy changes, as opposed to reforms in external communications, which preclude public diplomacy initiatives. The EU, as always, has not remained passive to critiques and has undertaken new strategies to respond to them.

To show publics that the EU us aware of their confusion and desires for change, EU public diplomacy has been promoting and highlighting its new attempts at unification of voice and action, and at utilizing its smart power, bolstered especially by the long-awaited ratification of the Lisbon Treaty. This is evidenced in a December 2009 article, by Commissioner Ferrero-Waldner, in which she stressed the need for "a European Union which thinks and acts globally, which speaks with one voice and pools its strengths, and which pursues a truly common external policy."112 EU leaders are not blind to the world's criticism and their frank words confirm the EU's admission that it needs to reform the way it conducts foreign relations by centralizing and unifying its voice.

The Lisbon Treaty has been promoted as the solution to many of the EU's perceived problems in terms of unification and cohesive communication and action. EU leaders have come out excitedly praising the treaty, including Commission President Barroso, who stated that after the treaty's "difficult birth," "all the pieces of the jigsaw are in place for a qualitative leap in the transatlantic relationship."113 While reaffirming the EU's awareness of a respite in U.S.-EU relations, the EU, via Barroso, offers the treaty as the solution, conveying that the EU is not only aware of the U.S.' grievances but has also taken steps to mollify them. The posts of President of the European Council and the High Representative of the Union for Foreign Affairs and Security Policy have been presented as solutions to the EU's difficulties of speaking and acting collectively.

Commissioner Ashton, upon taking up her new post of High Representative, wasted no time proclaiming it her job "… to make our voice stronger and more unified."115 In her first major security policy speech, to the Munich Security Conference, Ashton speaks of mobilizing all the EU's levers of influence - political, economic, plus civil and military crisis-management tools - in support of a single political strategy."116 In this way, she presents all of the EU's capabilities equally, while affirming that they will be unified to present one strategy to the world. She also mentions the EEAS as the manifestation of the EU's "joined-up thinking."

The diplomatic corps is presented as a solution to the EU's lack of a unified voice, as exhibited by the various and, at times, disjointed external communications of the member nations. As the EU's voice, Ashton reiterated the rhetoric of unity built around the new reforms of the Lisbon Treaty to show the world that the EU is actively making reforms to become a single actor. While the EU has also undertaken the task of tapping into its smart power capabilities, combining soft and hard power, its public diplomacy has been given the task of promoting this, using EU leaders to openly persuade publics of the EU's military strength; to see the EU as more than an economic and or cultural power, but as a multi-faceted global power. As early as 2007, the EU's external relations website mentioned defence as an important part of the EU's bid to bring world stability.

The EU was already aware of the changing global power structure as a result of wars and weapons acquisitions and took steps to assert its place in the realm of security. More recently, it has shown an awareness of the marginalization of its soft power in the wake of the economic crisis, and has taken steps to publicize its military capabilities.118 Wallstrom states that the EU model has not been one exclusively based on soft power by listing examples of the EU's use of member states' militaries to support its humanitarian and democracy promotion efforts[83].

---

[83] Bouquet, Dorothee Marie. ""Un-Patriotic" Knowledge: Diplomacy in Modern Language Education in France and in the United States, 1900-1939." Order No. 3543375, Purdue University, 2012. In PROQUESTMS ProQuest Dissertations & Theses Full Text,

These include support of the elections in the Democratic Republic of Congo as well as deployment of troops to the capital to safeguard the process; supplying humanitarian aid to the victims of the Tsunami in Indonesia, while putting in place "a military-backed peace process that enabled guerrillas to put down their guns and go home;" and supporting Moldova's efforts to reform, while stationing police on its border to combat smuggling." She shows that even without its own military force, the EU, through that of its members, is able to be a relevant defence actor. Wallstrom confirms that through its Foreign Security Policy, the EU is slowly moving to guide its hard power towards its international policy objectives, "when all other options fail."

In showing hard power as a last resort option, Wallstrom makes sure to convey that soft power is still very much a large part of the EU's repertoire and that it does not intend to abandon it, but rather continue to combine it with its hard power. In a different article, Ferrero-Waldner praises the European Neighbourhood Policy (ENP) as an example of the EU's smart power, listing all the aspects, in the service of both soft and hard power, the policy encompasses, like democratization assistance and defence aid.121 In his speech, Barroso directly answers critics of the EU's lack of engagement with the U.S.'s anti-terrorism initiatives when he reiterates the EU's involvement in

http://search.proquest.com/docview/1176562490?accountid=12085.

Afghanistan and Pakistan as a foreshadowing of more to come, since "the EU and the U.S. are just at the beginning of a more dynamic partnership in dealing with security challenges."

This again conveys that the EU has always been aware of a need for military strength, though has chosen to rely on its soft power instead. Now that the world needs it, the EU has and will continue to offer military aid, especially to its long-time partners like the U.S. These officials' clear statements in the service of public diplomacy reiterate the EU's new aims at correcting its mistake of relying too long on its cultural capital and signal the move to a more open and aware EU, willing to accept, and even implement, constructive criticism.

Recommendations

It is true that the EU member states' often lack of agreement on EU policies and actions limits its public diplomacy, but this is because the characterization of the EU as a nation-state leads to expectations of a categorical unity across all issues. The EU must move away from the generally accepted view that its public diplomacy is fractured because of its structure and, instead, must see the advantages of its novel structure, and communicate them to publics. In fact, some even consider the EU's public diplomacy better adapted to the fluidity of international relations and the pursuit of EU objectives than a more traditional organization with a single voice.

An unconventional institution like the EU must employ an unconventional public diplomacy strategy. Its focus should move away from proving that the EU is integrated, and more to highlighting how, with 27 member states, the EU is still able to make effective policy decisions without stifling the member states' separate identities. It is up to public diplomacy to reframe the image of the EU from an incoherent and discordant institution, lacking in military power, to that of an unprecedented global achievement in governance and security that is, and always will be, a work in progress, so that its many voice may be seen as unique benefits. It must promote a new classification of itself as a supranational institution, which leaves room for, and even welcomes, different voices. EU public diplomacy practitioners must be fully aware of the challenge of explaining and garnering credibility for such a novel classification.142 This is why EU public diplomacy must present an honest picture of the various aspects of such a characterization, highlighting positive aspects of the EU and showing how, by using the distinct tools at its disposal, it is making strides in changing the way the world thinks about international relations.

Change in Approach

EU public diplomacy must educate publics as to the true image and identity if the EU: a collection of different, separate voices which have come together for mutual benefit, to serve as an example of solidarity and good governance, who are, at the same time, able to maintain their distinct characteristics and identities. EU public diplomacy must make it a priority to reorient the public's characterization of the EU as a nation-state by highlighting the EU's distinct characteristics which separate it from a nation-state as evidence for the need for a new set of standards and, therefore, the new classification of a supranational institution. It would be most useful to introduce this term into its communications, making sure to thoroughly explain and define it, so that its usage increases and, overtime, it becomes part of the global lexicon.

By pioneering the use of this term, the EU can shape the public's understanding and maintain the role of expert over its use. Instead of constantly communicating the unity rhetoric, EU public diplomacy must do a better job of acknowledging its varied composition. It is important for the EU to communicate its differences from a nation-state, thereby, separating itself from its members, yet it must be aware that in doing so, it creates confusion; a confusion which can be helped with promotion of the EU's identity as a supranational institution.

EU and its Members: One Voice Does Not Apply

The EU and its members must view each others' public diplomacies as mutually beneficial. To achieve this, they must build transparent and collaborative public diplomacy partnerships. Instead of vying for attention with individual member states' public diplomacy efforts, EU public diplomacy must integrate them more dynamically into its own endeavours. By partnering on public diplomacy initiatives, something that has already been done on a small scale, it will show the member states that it is not trying to take over but rather enhance their relationships with non-EU countries. In this way, it will benefit from the expertise, resources and existing relationships of EU countries' public diplomacy, and ensure a double platform for its communications.

For their part, member states, while maintaining their public diplomacy voices, must be more pro-active in educating publics about their EU membership and new identities as members. Using the public's affinity for EU members' cultural aspects, public diplomacy should promote the construction of the new culture of the EU as a salad, not a melting pot, of the nations' distinct cultures, underlining the members' retention of their distinct characteristics coupled with an openness to new influences. It is important to counteract the image of the member states as constantly fighting to be heard by presenting the ways that they have maintained, and even complimented, their sovereignty as a benefit of EU membership.

To do this, EU public diplomacy must more readily and openly present their separate voices, acknowledging and supporting them. One way of doing this is through the promotion of the reforms under the Lisbon Treaty that allow for more state involvement in the decision making processes of the EU. This would foster the image of the EU as an inclusive entity and connect it more seamlessly to the images of the member states. By bringing to light this equal relationship, the EU's voice will be seen not in opposition to its members, but as a complement. It is also important for EU public diplomacy initiatives to show that the EU is different from its member states, in that while the EU represents, as a whole, the views of its members, its members, as individuals, do not necessarily represent the views of the EU.

The proliferation of different voices across the EU spectrum should not be viewed as a detriment, but should instead be promoted as a unique characteristic beneficial to the EU's continued success in directly representing its members. In understanding the EU as a supranational institution, publics should reject the one-voice scenario as irrelevant for the EU because it is not a nation state, but rather a collection of nation states with separate voices. The public should be made aware that public diplomacy has room for varied voices because there is so much distinct cultural capital across the EU that, at times, individual member states are more adapt at promoting it than the EU.

As for the new EEAS, the diplomatic corps, as representatives of the EU, must collaborate with member nations' representatives with the understanding that their goals are not in opposition, but rather, interlaced. Embassies and delegations must combine their efforts to not only show the world a united front, but also to increase their resources and capabilities in host countries. At the same time, member state representations and embassies need not disappear, as their existence is testament to the EU's allowance, and even need, for individual identities.

EU as a Role Model

Another task facing EU public diplomacy is the reinvigoration of the eroding role of the EU "as a social model to be imitated." First, in promoting a new characterization of the EU as a supranational institution, public diplomacy has the potential to stake out a separate niche for itself in the public's consciousness, apart from any other entities. With this in mind, EU public diplomacy must portray the EU as a positive force for reform in the way that states and institutions conduct inter and intra state relations. Publics should view it as a model for other, similar, institutions as well as all international actors.

Public diplomacy should focus on how, "Despite the barbarity of wars and devastating national rivalries, the people of Europe have managed to build a zone of peace, democracy, freedom and prosperity the like of which mankind had never seen before." While the U.S. and its development is similar to the EU model, the individual identities and the language differences of EU members serve as distinguishing points. The EU stands as an extraordinary achievement in economic and political integration. Its 27 distinct members, as well as the several others waiting anxiously to join, serve as a testament to its strength as a normative power.

Its ability to lead political and economic reforms, especially in countries of the former Soviet Union, is made even more extraordinary by the fact that its coercive mechanisms have relied on non-aggressive tactics. Public diplomacy should highlight the EU's achievements in overcoming nationalism and neo-colonialism, as well as its dual embrace of integration through unity and diversity through enlargement. Its brand of diversity due to its varied composition is unlike any in the world and is a testament to its citizens' growing acceptance of different publics, eroding characterizations of Europeans as discriminating and elitist. The member state's transition to the EU governance structure while preserving individual sovereignty can best be conveyed through more collaborative projects between the EU and member states in third countries. This way, publics can witness, first hand, the dynamic partnerships at work.

Public diplomacy should employ tools of contrast and comparison to convey the message of EU distinction, positing the EU of the present with the Europe of the past, to show how far the union and its individual members have come. The EU's public diplomacy strategy must centre on education and transparency, presenting the EU in a more sincere and, perhaps, vulnerable light. By admitting its faults and failures, the EU will show the world a more honest image, not shying away from the occasional lack of coherence and adding to the novelty and distinction of a picture of the EU as an experiment and a work in progress. Such honesty and vulnerability will actually make publics more accepting and forgiving of the EU's struggles and endear the EU to them.

EU as a Learning Process

In line with a more honest representation of the EU, EU public diplomacy should present the EU as a learning process; a blending and testing of ideas about governance. As an experiment in international governance, the EU should be seen as an evolving institution, constantly looking for ways to streamline and improve.148 As an "unfinished political system,"149 the EU has more room for maneuvering and fluidity. Through this kind of portrayal, its constant reforms should be seen as a testament to its commitment to achieving the best possible model of governance, adding to its image as role model and innovator. While a large part of public diplomacy already communicates new reforms and policies, this should be reframed, not as an attempt to conform the EU to the expectations of others, or as a symbol of the EU's lack of coherence, but as part of its constant self reevaluation and improvement.

In being open about the bumps in the road, EU public diplomacy will be more in line with the realities and actions of the EU, and therefore gain more credibility. Admitting the EU's inconsistencies and disagreements will allow its achievements to be framed in terms of unprecedented progress in the realm of global integration, adding to its role model identity. The EU has exhibited its awareness of this, most recently, by Barroso's acknowledgement of the EU members' divergence of opinion on the SWIFT Agreement, reached in 2009, between the EU and the U.S. to allow access to U.S. law enforcement authorities to the payment database of the financial consortium SWIFT. While he acknowledged and called for respect for the differing opinions in the EU on this topic of privacy, he also reiterated that this does not have to mean delay, adding that the EU has already presented a negotiating mandate to the member states.

This approach shows the EU's honesty about the realities of its unique composition and the challenges it presents, while showing that the challenges are being overcome. Publics must be treated as informed actors privy to the disagreements and inconsistencies within the EU. Covering this up with an image of a cohesive multilateral institution only makes the EU dishonest and exposes and highlights inconsistencies. Letting the world know that the EU is, and continues to be, an experiment in global governance will prompt publics to move away from focusing on the negative to seeing the actions of the EU in a new light, as examples of its identity as an innovator. As a new kind of supranational institution, the EU should be presented as a leader, faced with challenges, but forging ahead. With a new, more honest tone, EU public diplomacy should be open about the challenges the EU faces, even acknowledging others' critiques and why and how they do not pertain to the EU's true identity.

EU as A Soft Power

Instead of trying to adopt and foster an image, like many of its counterparts in the world, of a militarily strong actor, the EU should continue to foster the image which has continued to garner it support and favourable standing in the world, using its new identity of supranationality as reason for this divergence. Though there is some advantage to being a hard power in the world, this advantage is fleeting, and rests on one's constant ability to reassert one's strength. In contrast, soft power, when focused on cultivating dialogue and fostering partnerships is more constant and permanent, much more advantageous in the long term. Copeland opines that the EU has no place for hard power as this will not be the mark of dominance in an increasingly multipolar world.

While this is a rather radical view, it underscores the importance of not succumbing to the world's obsession with military might, as this will not last. While national security should remain a significant issue for the EU, its public diplomacy need not highlight the EU's military strength, as this takes away from its image as a unique actor. The EU's public diplomacy is much better off not focusing on the attempts to devise a common defence policy and continuing to harness the EU's soft power. Under its new classification as a supranational institution, public diplomacy must give more credibility to the unique attributes of the EU.

Its economic strength will bring political influence, and, eventually, international clout. With its peace, prosperity, safe and livable cities, social safety net, excellent public infrastructure, rich historical heritage and thriving artistic and cultural life, in the era of heteropolarity, Europa seems destined to lead the world in soft power, the power of attraction. The source of Europe's strength and the basis of its comparative advantage will reside in the demonstration effect, in the ability to project its success by example internationally. The EU, in its attempts to assert its military power, especially in the present time of heightened awareness of the dangers of war, is only eroding its face as a peaceful actor in an increasingly chaotic world.

EU public diplomacy has so much in its smart power arsenal that far outweighs asserting its military muscle, like its vast humanitarian aid, democracy promotion and cultural capital, that there is no need to resort to controversial actions which are out of its character. Its subtle approach to power assertion is much more affective, long-lasting and, more importantly, does not wane with its ability to exert force. The crucial public diplomacy goal of building relationships will present itself much more easily to the EU under the non-menacing image cultivated by its soft power-heavy approach, than under the hostile image often evoked through hard power. Relationships built on shared values, like those of the EU members, should be brought to light as more sustaining and mutually beneficial than ones struck out of fear or dependence.

EU public diplomacy must champion the move away from the perception that military force is somehow associated with strength. It must promote itself as the first global power, while having the capabilities to do so, actively chooses not maintain a collective military force. It may do so by highlighting the lack of war between any EU countries since their ascension into the union with a celebration of an anniversary every year. By promoting the EU as a force for change, public diplomacy will usher in the idea of a new kind of strength, based on the ability to influence global norms; one that is far more stoic than strength derived from military power. Furthermore, in the competition for the public's attention in an increasingly information saturated environment, the EU, vis-à- vis its soft power, would garner more lasting attention as a nonconformist. Such an approach underlines the EU's unique identity as a leader among followers: while everyone resorts to flashing their weapons, the EU, by flashing peace signs, champions a new approach.

BIBLIOGRAPHY

Abdel Samei, Marwa. "Public Diplomacy in the Age of Regional Media: Winning the War of Hearts and Minds in the Middle East AL-Jazeera and Al-Hurra." Order No. 3411814, Northeastern University, 2010. In PROQUESTMS ProQuest Dissertations & Theses Full Text, http://search.proquest.com/docview/649191171?accou ntid=12085.

Aden, Ubah A. "The Birth of Post-War U.S. Government Propaganda: The Truman Administration and its Ideological Struggle with the Union of Soviet Socialist Republics (USSR)." Order No. 1509516, Georgetown University, 2012. In PROQUESTMS ProQuest Dissertations & Theses Full Text, http://search.proquest.com/docview/1013827223?acco untid=12085.

Albritton, R. B., & Manheim, J. B. News of Rhodesia: The impact of a public relations campaign. Journalism Quarterly, 60, 622-628. (1983).

Asmolov, Grigori (Gregory). "The Development of Network Diplomacy: A Comparative Analysis---Israel, the U.S., and Russia." Order No. 1476755, The George Washington University, 2010. In PROQUESTMS ProQuest Dissertations & Theses Full Text, http://search.proquest.com/docview/516237660?accou ntid=12085.

Ball-Rokeach, S. Media system dependency theory. In M. DeFleur, & S. Ball- Rokeach (Eds.), Theories of mass communication. (5th ed.). New York: Longman. (1979).

Bell, Aryn Elizabeth. "Elizabeth I and the Policy of Marriage: The Anjou Match, 1572-1582." Order No. 1541624, The University of North Dakota, 2013. In PROQUESTMS ProQuest Dissertations & Theses Full Text, http://search.proquest.com/docview/1418750925?acco untid=12085.

Bennett, W. L. Toward a theory of press-state relations in the United States. Journal of Communication, 40 (2), 103–125. (1990).

Berkout, Olga Vadymovna. "Impact of Relationship Context on Evaluations of the Sexual Behavior of Men and Women." Order No. 1495765, The University of Mississippi, 2011. In PROQUESTMS ProQuest Dissertations & Theses Full Text, http://search.proquest.com/docview/880487761?accountid=12085.

Blaustein, George Holt, Jr. "To the Heart of Europe: Americanism, the Salzburg Seminar, and Cultural Diplomacy." Order No. 3395409, Harvard University, 2010. In PROQUESTMS ProQuest Dissertations & Theses Full Text, http://search.proquest.com/docview/305213248?accountid=12085.

Boulding, K. E. National images and international systems. In J. N. Rosenau (Ed.), International politics and foreign policy (pp. 422-431). New York: The Free Press. (1969).

Boulding, K. E. The image. Ann Arbor: University of Michigan Press. (1956).

Bouquet, Dorothee Marie. ""Un-Patriotic" Knowledge: Diplomacy in Modern Language Education in France and in the United States, 1900-1939." Order No. 3543375, Purdue University, 2012. In PROQUESTMS ProQuest Dissertations & Theses Full Text, http://search.proquest.com/docview/1176562490?accountid=12085.

Brodsky, Lauren Naomi. "Democracy Across the Airwaves: The Strategic Work of American International Broadcasting in Azerbaijan and Iran." Order No. 3422072, Fletcher School of Law and Diplomacy (Tufts University), 2010. In PROQUESTMS ProQuest Dissertations & Theses Full Text, http://search.proquest.com/docview/755479271?accountid=12085.

Brown, Jessica Arin. "Islam, the United States and Multiple Identities: An Analysis of Determinants of Muslim Public Opinion of the United States and its Implications for U.S. Public Diplomacy." Order No. 1475294, Georgetown University, 2010. In PROQUESTMS ProQuest Dissertations & Theses Full Text, http://search.proquest.com/docview/276391400?accou ntid=12085.

Budabin, Alexandra Cosima. "Citizens' Army for Darfur the Impact of a Social Movement on International Conflict Resolution." Order No. 3495816, New School University, 2012. In PROQUESTMS ProQuest Dissertations & Theses Full Text, http://search.proquest.com/docview/924490309?accou ntid=12085.

Buddenhagen, Caroline Riker. "Fine Line Or Hard Line? the Tension between Security and Public Diplomacy in Visa Policy before and After 9/11." Order No. 1556256, Georgetown University, 2013. In PROQUESTMS ProQuest Dissertations & Theses Full Text, http://search.proquest.com/docview/1540813427?acco untid=12085.

Butts, Robert H. "An Architect of the American Century: Colonel Edward M. House and the Modernization of United States Diplomacy." Order No. 3443311, Texas Christian University, 2010. In PROQUESTMS ProQuest Dissertations & Theses Full Text, http://search.proquest.com/docview/854839987?accou ntid=12085.

Carlson, Joana Renee. "Blurring the Boundaries of Cold War Foreign Relations: Popular Diplomacy, Transnationalism, and U.S. Policy Toward Post-Revolutionary China and Cuba." Order No. 3462283, The Florida State University, 2010. In PROQUESTMS ProQuest Dissertations & Theses Full Text, http://search.proquest.com/docview/875962580?accou ntid=12085.

Chahhou, Khalid. "The Status of Languages in Post-Independent Morocco: Moroccan National Policies and Spanish Cultural Action." Order No. 3641830, City University of New York, 2014. In PROQUESTMS ProQuest Dissertations & Theses Full Text, http://search.proquest.com/docview/1623001438?acco untid=12085.

Chahine, Joumane. "Public Diplomacy: A Conceptual Framework." Order No. NR61976, McGill University (Canada), 2011. In PROQUESTMS ProQuest Dissertations & Theses Full Text, http://search.proquest.com/docview/902903290?accou ntid=12085.

Chang, T. All countries not created equal to be news: World system and international communication. Communication Research, 25 (5), 528-563. (1998).

Cheng, Zhuqing. "An Examination of the First- and Second-Level of Agenda Building with the Image of China's President Xi Jinping in Xinhua and Four U.S. News Outlets." Order No. 1564859, Syracuse University, 2014. In PROQUESTMS ProQuest Dissertations & Theses Full Text, http://search.proquest.com/docview/1615884246?acco untid=12085.

Choi, Suh Hee. "Conceptualizing Tourism Image and Nation Image: An Integrated Relational-Behavioral Model." Order No. 3507221, Purdue University, 2011. In PROQUESTMS ProQuest Dissertations & Theses Full Text, http://search.proquest.com/docview/1015364634?acco untid=12085.

Christenson, Joel C. "From Gunboats to Good Neighbors: U.S. Naval Diplomacy in Peru, 1919-1942." Order No. 3571567, West Virginia University, 2013. In PROQUESTMS ProQuest Dissertations & Theses Full Text, http://search.proquest.com/docview/1426846310?acco untid=12085.

Cole, Randy Edward, Jr. "The Rhetorical Turn in United States Diplomacy Praxis: Public Diplomacy 2.0." Order No. 3557833, Duquesne University, 2013. In PROQUESTMS ProQuest Dissertations & Theses Full Text, http://search.proquest.com/docview/1346683978?acco untid=12085.

Coleman, R., & Banning, S. Network TV news' affective framing of the presidential candidates: Evidence for a second-level agenda-setting effect through visual framing. Journalism and Mass Communication Quarterly, 83 (2), 313-328. (2006).

Colona,William T.,,II. "Social Media and the Advancement of America's Soft Power by Public Diplomacy." Order No. 1508114, Georgetown University, 2012. In PROQUESTMS ProQuest Dissertations & Theses Full Text, http://search.proquest.com/docview/968947391?accou ntid=12085.

Crisp, Jeremy D. "Media Framing, Proximity and Spheres: The Media Account before and After the August 21, 2013 Syrian Chemical Attack." Order No. 1553276, Gonzaga University, 2013. In PROQUESTMS ProQuest Dissertations & Theses Full Text, http://search.proquest.com/docview/1513235496?acco untid=12085.

De Santo, Paola Chiara. ""(Ne) Habeas Corpus": The Body and the Body Politic in the Figures of the Ambassador and the Courtesan in Renaissance Italy." Order No. 3626550, Harvard University, 2014. In PROQUESTMS ProQuest Dissertations & Theses Full Text, http://search.proquest.com/docview/1557754017?acco untid=12085.

Dempsey, Michael Matthew. "Champion of Two Worlds: A Phenomenological Investigation of North Carolina Early College Liaisons' Leadership Experiences." Order No. 3588961, Western Carolina University, 2013. In PROQUESTMS ProQuest Dissertations &

Theses   Full   Text,
http://search.proquest.com/docview/1428738850?acco
untid=12085.

Diawara, Marieme A. "Islam and Public Health: French Management of the Hajj from Colonial Senegal and Muslim Responses Beginning in 1895." Order No. 3504135, Michigan State University, 2012. In PROQUESTMS ProQuest Dissertations & Theses Full Text, http://search.proquest.com/docview/1010783877?acco untid=12085.

Donos, Maxim. "Communicating Sport Mega-Events and the Soft Power Dimensions of Public Diplomacy." Order No. MR86488, University of Ottawa (Canada), 2012. In PROQUESTMS ProQuest Dissertations & Theses Full   Text, http://search.proquest.com/docview/1356818844?acco untid=12085.

Dougherty, Jill. "Russia's "Soft Power" Strategy." Order No. 1556260, Georgetown University, 2013. In PROQUESTMS ProQuest Dissertations & Theses Full Text, http://search.proquest.com/docview/1540812881?acco untid=12085.

Duchemin, Michael Dean. "New Deal Cowboy: Gene Autry and Public Diplomacy." Order No. 3523669, University of Nevada, Las Vegas, 2012. In PROQUESTMS ProQuest Dissertations & Theses Full Text, http://search.proquest.com/docview/1038158542?acco untid=12085.

Eibl, Marita. "PEPFAR, Politics, and Patients / Antiretroviral Treatment in Tanzania." Order No. 3435232, Michigan State University, 2010. In PROQUESTMS ProQuest Dissertations   &   Theses   Full   Text, http://search.proquest.com/docview/816030283?accou ntid=12085.

Elliot, Daniel J. "Exploring the Relationship between Educational Inequality and Group-Level Armed

Conflict within a Country." Order No. 1554554, Georgetown University, 2014. In PROQUESTMS ProQuest Dissertations & Theses Full Text, http://search.proquest.com/docview/1528531200?acco untid=12085.

Faith, Robert. "Rescuing Trade from Necessity: Henry Kissinger's Economic Diplomacy Toward the Soviet Union." Order No. 1498493, Indiana University of Pennsylvania, 2011. In PROQUESTMS ProQuest Dissertations & Theses Full Text, http://search.proquest.com/docview/894086273?accou ntid=12085.

Fisk, Matthew Henry. "Paradox of Elitism: Vision, Risk, and Diplomacy in the European Career of Colonel John Trumbull (1756-1843)." Order No. 3559788, University of California, Santa Barbara, 2013. In PROQUESTMS ProQuest Dissertations & Theses Full Text, http://search.proquest.com/docview/1354501667?acco untid=12085.

Fouladvand, Hida. "Public Diplomacy Gangnam Style." Order No. 1556438, Georgetown University, 2014. In PROQUESTMS ProQuest Dissertations & Theses Full Text, http://search.proquest.com/docview/1539537560?acco untid=12085.

Frederick, H. Global communication and international relations. Belmont, CA: Wadsworth. (1993).

Froh, David. "Soft Power, Constructivism and the Rwandan Genocide." Order No. MR88566, The University of Regina (Canada), 2010. In PROQUESTMS ProQuest Dissertations & Theses Full Text, http://search.proquest.com/docview/1064955196?acco untid=12085.

Gagnon, Michelle Leona. "Global Health Diplomacy: Understanding how and Why Health is Integrated into Foreign Policy." Order No. NR98101, University of Ottawa (Canada), 2012. In PROQUESTMS ProQuest Dissertations & Theses Full Text,

http://search.proquest.com/docview/1356851849?acco
untid=12085.

Galtung, J., & Ruge, M. H. The structure of foreign news. Journal of Peace Research, 2 (1), 64-91. (1965).

Gary, David J. "Rufus King and the History of Reading: The use of Print in the Early American Republic." Order No. 3553074, City University of New York, 2013. In PROQUESTMS ProQuest Dissertations & Theses Full Text, http://search.proquest.com/docview/1314577167?acco untid=12085.

Ghanem, S. Filling the tapestry: The second-level of agenda-setting. In M. McCombs, D. L. Shaw, & D. Weaver (Eds.), Communication and democracy: Exploring the intellectual frontiers in agenda-setting theory (pp. 3-27). Mahwah, NJ: Lawrence Erlbaum Associates.

Gilboa, E. Mass communication and diplomacy: A theoretical framework. Communication Theory, 10 (3), 275-309. (2000).

Ginzburg, Lyubov. "Confronting the Cold War Legacy: The Forgotten History of the American Colony in St Petersburg a Case Study of Reconciliation." Order No. 3409068, University of Kansas, 2010. In PROQUESTMS ProQuest Dissertations & Theses Full Text, http://search.proquest.com/docview/612741904?accou ntid=12085.

Golan, G., & Wanta, W. Second-level agenda-setting in the New Hampshire primary: A comparison of coverage in three newspapers and public perceptions of candidates. Journalism and Mass Communication Quarterly, 78 (2), 247-259. (2001).

Gottfried, Matthew Stuart. "The Origins and Consequences of Public Opinion in Coercive Terrorist Crises." Order No. 3621755, University of California, Los Angeles, 2014. In PROQUESTMS ProQuest Dissertations & Theses Full Text, http://search.proquest.com/docview/1545890466?acco untid=12085.

Gu, Yao. "Byron's "Don Juan" and Nationalism." Order No. 3436617, The Chinese University of Hong Kong (Hong Kong), 2010. In PROQUESTMS ProQuest Dissertations & Theses Full Text, http://search.proquest.com/docview/822408732?accou ntid=12085.

Guenette, Salam. "Franco-British Diplomatic Relations Transformed? the Socio-Political Impact of the Emigres' Presence in Britain." Order No. MS26421, University of Victoria (Canada), 2013. In PROQUESTMS ProQuest Dissertations & Theses Full Text, http://search.proquest.com/docview/1520225582?acco untid=12085.

Gummer, S. C. "The Politics of Sympathy: German Turcophilism and the Ottoman Empire in the Age of the Mass Media 1871--1914." Order No. 3433144, Georgetown University, 2011. In PROQUESTMS ProQuest Dissertations & Theses Full Text, http://search.proquest.com/docview/835067334?accou ntid=12085.

Hall, Christa Marie. "Peace Corps to the Right: An Analysis of the U.S. Peace Corps in Central America." Order No. 1491414, Georgetown University, 2011. In PROQUESTMS ProQuest Dissertations & Theses Full Text, http://search.proquest.com/docview/865808684?accou ntid=12085.

Han, Ji Yoon. "National Reputation by a Non-Profit Organization: How Voluntary Agency Network of Korea (VANK) Affects the National Reputation of South Korea." Order No. 1518805, Syracuse University, 2012. In PROQUESTMS ProQuest Dissertations & Theses Full Text, http://search.proquest.com/docview/1069261854?acco untid=12085.

Harmes, David T. "International Radio Broadcasting and Post-Conflict State-Building: The Case of Canada's Rana FM." Order No. NR93370, Ryerson University

(Canada), 2012. In PROQUESTMS ProQuest Dissertations & Theses Full Text, http://search.proquest.com/docview/1350628046?acco untid=12085.

Harris, Richard J. "Ambassador Doraemon: Japan's Pop Culture Diplomacy in China and South Korea." Order No. 1508566, Georgetown University, 2012. In PROQUESTMS ProQuest Dissertations & Theses Full Text, http://search.proquest.com/docview/1010625651?acco untid=12085.

Jalali, Javad. "The Impact of Sanctions upon Civil Aviation Safety." Order No. MR83973, McGill University (Canada), 2011. In PROQUESTMS ProQuest Dissertations & Theses Full Text, http://search.proquest.com/docview/1033333572?acco untid=12085.

Jervis, R. The logic of images in international relations. Princeton, NJ: Princeton University Press. (1970).

Keess, John. "Defence, Diplomacy and Discord: The Impact of the Great War and its Effect on Canadian Strategy, 1920--1928." Order No. MR89109, University of New Brunswick (Canada), 2011. In PROQUESTMS ProQuest Dissertations & Theses Full Text, http://search.proquest.com/docview/1153964715?acco untid=12085.

Khakimova, Leysan. "An Exploratory Study of the Meaning of Public Diplomacy: Network Approach." Order No. 3599613, University of Maryland, College Park, 2013. In PROQUESTMS ProQuest Dissertations & Theses Full Text, http://search.proquest.com/docview/1461770763?acco untid=12085.

Khamidov, Alisher. "The Base of Contention: Kyrgyzstan, Russia and the U.S. in Central Asia (2001--2010)." Order No. 3483028, The Johns Hopkins University, 2011. In PROQUESTMS ProQuest Dissertations & Theses Full Text,

http://search.proquest.com/docview/902627242?accou
ntid=12085.

Kim, Y. Measuring the economic value of public relations.
Public Relations Research, 13 (1), 3-26. (2001).

Kinstetter, Gregory A. "Let Poland be Poland." Order No.
1510007, University of Wyoming, 2012. In
PROQUESTMS ProQuest Dissertations & Theses Full
Text,
http://search.proquest.com/docview/1015032502?acco
untid=12085.

Klein, Adam Gordon. "A Quiet Road to War: Media
Compliance and Suppressed Public Opinion in Iran."
Order No. 3402791, Howard University, 2010. In
PROQUESTMS ProQuest Dissertations & Theses Full
Text,
http://search.proquest.com/docview/305212388?accou
ntid=12085.

Koster, Karleigh. "Pioneers of the Global University:
Participant Experience and Study Abroad in
Midwestern Public Higher Education from the Cold
War to the Present." Order No. 3567291, New York
University, 2013. In PROQUESTMS ProQuest
Dissertations & Theses Full Text,
http://search.proquest.com/docview/1417775979?acco
untid=12085.

Krzakowski, Caroline Zoe. "Aftermath: Foreign Relations and
the Postwar British Novel." Order No. NR78789,
McGill University (Canada), 2012. In PROQUESTMS
ProQuest Dissertations & Theses Full Text,
http://search.proquest.com/docview/1151101458?acco
untid=12085.

Labinski, Nicholas. "Evolution of a President: John F. Kennedy
and Berlin." Order No. 1496774, Marquette
University, 2011. In PROQUESTMS ProQuest
Dissertations & Theses Full Text,
http://search.proquest.com/docview/890109254?accou
ntid=12085.

Larson, J. F. International affairs coverage on U.S. evening
news networks news. In W. C. Adams (Ed.),

Television coverage of international affairs (pp. 15-39). Norwood, NJ: Ablex Publishing Co. (1982).

Lavender, Wayne. "Worldview and Public Policy: From American Exceptionalism to American Empire." Order No. 3399168, George Mason University, 2010. In PROQUESTMS ProQuest Dissertations & Theses Full Text, http://search.proquest.com/docview/219894411?accou ntid=12085.

Lee, S. A theoretical model of national image processing and international public relations. Unpublished doctoral dissertation. Syracuse University. (2004).

Libbey, J. K. & Goldberg, H. J. "The Sources of Soviet Conduct," Foreign Affairs, July 1947, Vol. 25, pp. 566-582. (1947)

Litvinsky, Marina. "European Union Public Diplomacy: The Need for a New Frame." Order No. 1477202, The George Washington University, 2010. In PROQUESTMS ProQuest Dissertations & Theses Full Text, http://search.proquest.com/docview/578504400?accou ntid=12085.

Loidolt, Bryce. "Terrorists Or Troublemakers? Regime Survival and Inflating the Al-Qaeda Threat." Order No. 1545096, The University of North Carolina at Chapel Hill, 2013. In PROQUESTMS ProQuest Dissertations & Theses Full Text, http://search.proquest.com/docview/1438853079?acco untid=12085.

Lu, Yanqin. "Do Netizens Overlook "Official Frames" in China a Framing Analysis of Online News and Micro-Blogging Posts." Order No. 1538573, Indiana University, 2013. In PROQUESTMS ProQuest Dissertations & Theses Full Text, http://search.proquest.com/docview/1373382149?acco untid=12085.

Mackey, Timothy Ken. "Global Governance and Diplomacy Solutions for Counterfeit Medicines." Order No. 3567710, University of California, San Diego, 2013. In

PROQUESTMS ProQuest Dissertations & Theses Full Text,
http://search.proquest.com/docview/1417990538?acco untid=12085.

Magu, Stephen Macharia. "Soft Power Strategies in US Foreign Policy: Assessing the Impact of Citizen Diplomacy on Foreign States' Behavior." Order No. 3579613, Old Dominion University, 2013. In PROQUESTMS ProQuest Dissertations & Theses Full Text, http://search.proquest.com/docview/1508332215?acco untid=12085.

Manheim, J. B. A model of agenda dynamics. In M. McLaughlin (Ed.), Communication Year Book, Vol. 10 (pp. 499-516). Beverly Hills, CA: Sage. (1987).

Manheim, J. B., & Albritton, R. B. Changing national images: International public relations and media agenda-setting. The American Political Science Review, 78 (3), 641-657. (1984).

Marinova, Nadejda Kirilova. "House of Lebanon: How Host States use Diasporas---the George W. Bush Administration and the Lebanese-American Lobby." Order No. 3466054, University of Southern California, 2011. In PROQUESTMS ProQuest Dissertations & Theses Full Text, http://search.proquest.com/docview/884339035?accou ntid=12085.

Martin, Clifton. "Preventing the Clash: Reexamining U.S. Public Diplomacy in the Middle East." Order No. 1520093, University of Denver, 2012. In PROQUESTMS ProQuest Dissertations & Theses Full Text,
http://search.proquest.com/docview/1113390760?acco untid=12085.

McCallum, Caleb Edward. "Soft Power in a Hard Country: American Cultural Diplomacy in Iran, 1950--1955." Order No. 1484702, University of Arkansas, 2010. In PROQUESTMS ProQuest Dissertations & Theses Full Text,

http://search.proquest.com/docview/305184767?accou
ntid=12085.

McCombs, M. E., & Shaw, D. L. The agenda-setting function
of mass media. The Public Opinion Quarterly, 36 (2),
176-187. (1972).

McCombs, M. E., Liamas, J. P., Lopez-Escobar, E., & Rey, F.
Candidate images in Spanish elections: Second-level
agenda-setting   effects.   Journalism   and   Mass
Communication Quarterly, 74, 703-717. (1977).

McEachern, Jaclyn O'Brien. "Diplomatic Activity in Service of
Papal Teaching: The Promotion of Religious Freedom
in Relations with Selected Islamic States during the
Pontificate of John Paul II." Order No. 3427675, The
Catholic   University   of   America,   2010.   In
PROQUESTMS ProQuest Dissertations & Theses Full
Text,
http://search.proquest.com/docview/815229484?accou
ntid=12085.

McGee, Anne E. "Military Soft Power is Not an Oxymoron:
Using Public Diplomacy Analytic Approaches to
Examine Goals and Effects of U.S. Military
Educational Exchange Programs." Order No. 3493881,
Georgetown University, 2011. In PROQUESTMS
ProQuest   Dissertations   &   Theses   Full   Text,
http://search.proquest.com/docview/920317000?accou
ntid=12085.

McNelly, J. T., & Izcaray, F. International news exposure and
images of nations. Journalism Quarterly, 63 (3), 546-
553. (1986).

Mearsheimer, J, Walt, S., "An Unnecessary War", Foreign
Policy,   No.   134,   Carnegie   Endowment   for
International Peace, pp. 50-59. (2003)

Melissen, J. The new public diplomacy: Between theory and
practice. In J. Melissen (Eds.), The new public
diplomacy: Soft power in international relations. New
York: Palgrave Macmillan. (2006).

Morgenthau, H. J. "Politics Among Nations: The Struggle for
Power and Peace". New York: Knopf. pp. n.a. 1973

Mutsaka, Chiedza Michelle. "Changing Foreign Public Perceptions through Culture Comparative Study of the Cultural Diplomacy of France and China in the Mekong Sub-Region." Order No. 1525312, Webster University, 2013. In PROQUESTMS ProQuest Dissertations & Theses Full Text, http://search.proquest.com/docview/1531128195?acco untid=12085.

Nagy, Zsolt. "Grand Delusions: Interwar Hungarian Cultural Diplomacy, 1918-1941." Order No. 3526146, The University of North Carolina at Chapel Hill, 2012. In PROQUESTMS ProQuest Dissertations & Theses Full Text, http://search.proquest.com/docview/1040729378?acco untid=12085.

Nam, Seungji. "Independent Diplomacy between North Korea and China Folllowing the 20th Communist Congress of the Soviet Union." Order No. 1479925, University of Southern California, 2010. In PROQUESTMS ProQuest Dissertations & Theses Full Text, http://search.proquest.com/docview/748231594?accou ntid=12085.

Nisbet, E. C., Nisbet, M. C., Scheufele, D. A., & Shanahan, J. E. Public diplomacy, television news, and Muslim opinion. Harvard International Journal of Press/Politics, 9 (2), 11-37. (2004).

Nye, J. S., Jr. Bound to lead: The changing nature of American power. New York: Basic Books. (1990).

Nye, J. S., Jr. Soft power: The means to success in world politics. New York: Public Affairs. (2004).

Oblinger, Anne L. "The Moral, Legal, and Diplomatic Implications of Drone Warfare in Pakistan." Order No. 1499634, Georgetown University, 2011. In PROQUESTMS ProQuest Dissertations & Theses Full Text, http://search.proquest.com/docview/896126865?accou ntid=12085.

Palkki, David Dean. "Deterring Saddam Hussein's Iraq: Domestic Audience Costs and Credibility Assessments in Theory and Practice." Order No. 3610480, University of California, Los Angeles, 2013. In PROQUESTMS ProQuest Dissertations & Theses Full Text, http://search.proquest.com/docview/1500437527?acco untid=12085.

Ramirez, Shawn Ling. "Accountability and International Conflict." Order No. 3600457, University of Rochester, 2013. In PROQUESTMS ProQuest Dissertations & Theses Full Text, http://search.proquest.com/docview/1465055637?acco untid=12085.

Ramsey, Shawn D. "Deliberative Rhetoric in the Twelfth Century: The Case for Eleanor of Aquitaine, Noblewomen, and the Ars Dictaminis." Order No. 3528912, Bowling Green State University, 2012. In PROQUESTMS ProQuest Dissertations & Theses Full Text, http://search.proquest.com/docview/1086351139?acco untid=12085.

Rimner, Steffen. "The Asian Origins of Global Narcotics Control, c. 1860-1909." Order No. 3627071, Harvard University, 2014. In PROQUESTMS ProQuest Dissertations & Theses Full Text, http://search.proquest.com/docview/1557746398?acco untid=12085.

Ripley, Charles. "Pathways to Peace, Progress, and Public Goods: Rethinking Regional Hegemony." Order No. 3559641, Arizona State University, 2013. In PROQUESTMS ProQuest Dissertations & Theses Full Text, http://search.proquest.com/docview/1353674019?acco untid=12085.

Robison, G. Flying under the radar: U.S. Cultural diplomacy in the Middle East. Project report of the USC Center on Public Diplomacy. Retrieved Feb. 21, 2007 from http://uscpublicdiplomacy.com/pdfs/Robison_-_Cultural_Diplomacy_July06.pdf. (2005).

Roszkowski, Anna. "United Nations Peacekeeping as an International Tool for the Maintenance of International Peace and Security: Has it Exceeded its Original Purpose with the Missions being Carried Out Today?" Order No. 1492871, Webster University, 2011. In PROQUESTMS ProQuest Dissertations & Theses Full Text, http://search.proquest.com/docview/862990348?accou ntid=12085.

Salwen, M. B., & Matera, F. Public salience of foreign nations. Journalism Quarterly, 69 (3), 623-632. (1992).

Schneider, C. P. Culture communicates: US diplomacy that works. In J. Melissen (Ed.), The new public diplomacy: Soft power in international relations. New York: Palgrave Macmillan. (2006).

Schumacher, Leslie Rogne. "A "Lasting Solution": The Eastern Question and British Imperialism, 1875-1878." Order No. 3523024, University of Minnesota, 2012. In PROQUESTMS ProQuest Dissertations & Theses Full Text, http://search.proquest.com/docview/1037992277?acco untid=12085.

Scott, Kendra U. "Embassies as Art Institutions Symbols of Exchange." Order No. 1509762, American University, 2012. In PROQUESTMS ProQuest Dissertations & Theses Full Text, http://search.proquest.com/docview/1015014627?acco untid=12085.

Semetko, H. A., Brzinski, J., Weaver, D., & Willnat, L. TV news and U.S. public opinion about foreign countries: The impact of exposure and attention. International Journal of Public Opinion Research, 4, 18-36. (1992).

Seo, Hyunjin. "Structure of National Image in the Age of Networks: An Empirical Analysis of Online Social Relations and Information use." Order No. 3437585, Syracuse University, 2010. In PROQUESTMS ProQuest Dissertations & Theses Full Text, http://search.proquest.com/docview/821864627?accou ntid=12085.

Sevin, Hasan Efe. "Making New Friends? Relational Public Diplomacy as a Foreign Policy Instrument." Order No. 3631071, American University, 2014. In PROQUESTMS ProQuest Dissertations & Theses Full Text, http://search.proquest.com/docview/1564442089?acco untid=12085.

Shoemaker, P. J. Gatekeeping. Newbury Park, CA: Sage. (1991).

Shoemaker, P. J., & Reese, S. D. Mediating the message: Theories of influences on mass media content. White Plains, New York: Longman. (1991).

Shoemaker, P. J., Danielian, L. H., & Brendlinger, N. Deviant acts, risky business, and U.S. interests: The newsworthiness of world events. Journalism Quarterly, 68, 781-795. (1991).

Smith, D. D. Mass communications and international image change. Journal of Conflict Resolution, 17 (1), 115-129. (1973).

Stapleton, Bradford Ian. "The Strategic Consequences of Military Quagmires: An Examination of War-Weariness Theory." Order No. 3637502, University of California, Los Angeles, 2014. In PROQUESTMS ProQuest Dissertations & Theses Full Text, http://search.proquest.com/docview/1617458330?acco untid=12085.

Stocking, S. H. Effect of public relations efforts on media visibility of organizations. Journalism Quarterly, 62 (2), 358-366, 450. (1985).

Tomlin, Gregory Michael. "The Fishbowl World: Edward R. Murrow, John F. Kennedy, and the Cold War." Order No. 3557553, The George Washington University, 2013. In PROQUESTMS ProQuest Dissertations & Theses Full Text, http://search.proquest.com/docview/1346182118?acco untid=12085.

Touloumi, Olga. "Architectures of Global Communication: Psychoacoustics, Acoustic Space, and the Total Environment, 1941-1970." Order No. 3627231,

Harvard University, 2014. In PROQUESTMS ProQuest Dissertations & Theses Full Text, http://search.proquest.com/docview/1557745167?acco untid=12085.

Trent, Deborah Lee. "Transnational, Trans-Sectarian Engagement: A Revised Approach to U.S. Public Diplomacy Toward Lebanon." Order No. 3524305, The George Washington University, 2012. In PROQUESTMS ProQuest Dissertations & Theses Full Text, http://search.proquest.com/docview/1038836409?acco untid=12085.

Tuch, H. N. Communicating with the world: U.S. public diplomacy overseas. New York: St. Martin's Press. (1990).

Turow, J. Public relations and news work: A neglected relationship. American Behavioral Scientist, 33 (1989), pp. 206–212.

Ubelaker, Lisa A. "The Impossible Americas: Argentina, Ecuador, and the Geography of U.S. Mass Media, 1938--1948." Order No. 3572007, Yale University, 2013. In PROQUESTMS ProQuest Dissertations & Theses Full Text, http://search.proquest.com/docview/1433929786?acco untid=12085.

Veisz, Elizabeth. ""Well-Dispos'd Savages": Elite Masculinity in Eighteenth-Century British Literature." Order No. 3443519, University of Maryland, College Park, 2010. In PROQUESTMS ProQuest Dissertations & Theses Full Text, http://search.proquest.com/docview/854984341?accou ntid=12085.

Vibber, Kelly S. "Advocates Or Adversaries? an Exploration of Communicative Actions of within-Border Foreign Publics and their Affect on the Host Country's Soft Power." Order No. 3636675, Purdue University, 2014. In PROQUESTMS ProQuest Dissertations & Theses Full Text,

http://search.proquest.com/docview/1615376857?acco
untid=12085.

Walt, S. "*International Relations: One World, Many Theories,*" Foreign Policy (Spring): 29–46. (1998)

Walt, S., "*The relationship between theory and Policy in international relations*", Kennedy School of Government, Harvard University, Cambridge, Massachusetts 02138; pp. 1-28. (2004)

Wang, J. Managing national reputation and international relations in the global era: Public diplomacy revisited. Public Relations Review, 32, 91-96. (2006).

Wang, Szuhai J. "Public Diplomacy and Organizational Conflict: A Study of Taiwanese Government Information Offices in the United States." Order No. 3430719, University of La Verne, 2010. In PROQUESTMS ProQuest Dissertations & Theses Full Text, http://search.proquest.com/docview/795221111?accou ntid=12085.

Wanta, W. The effects of dominant photographs: An agenda-setting experiment. Journalism and Mass Communication Quarterly, 65 (1), 107-111. (1988).

Wanta, W., & Hu, Y-W. The agenda-setting effects of international news coverage: An examination of differing news frames. International Journal of Public Opinion Research, 5, 250-264. (1993).

Wanta, W., Golan, G, & Lee, C. Agenda-setting and international news: Media influence on public perceptions of foreign nations. Journalism and Mass Communication Quarterly, 82 (2), 364-377. (2004).

Westrum, Andrew T. "Global Health Diplomacy: A Multi-Method Critical Success Factor Analysis." Order No. 3489120, Central Michigan University, 2011. In PROQUESTMS ProQuest Dissertations & Theses Full Text, http://search.proquest.com/docview/912382119?accou ntid=12085.

Wheeler, Anita C. "China's Public Diplomacy in Kenya: The Case of Chinese Language and Cultural Programs at

the University of Nairobi Confucius Institute." Order
No. 3513298, Howard University, 2012. In
PROQUESTMS ProQuest Dissertations & Theses Full
Text,
http://search.proquest.com/docview/1025695423?acco
untid=12085.

Williams, Wanda T. "The Western Hemisphere's Pandora's
Box: How Race, Communism, and the Roman
Catholic Church Influenced U.S. Foreign Diplomacy
with Duvalier's Haiti, 1969-1971." Order No.
1496472, Morgan State University, 2011. In
PROQUESTMS ProQuest Dissertations & Theses Full
Text,
http://search.proquest.com/docview/881638180?accou
ntid=12085.

Williamson, James Franklin. "Memory with "no Clear
Answers": Volkstrauertag, Opfer Des Faschismus, and
the Politics of Publicly Mourning the War Dead in
Germany, 1945--1972." Order No. 3606789, The
University of North Carolina at Chapel Hill, 2013. In
PROQUESTMS ProQuest Dissertations & Theses Full
Text,
http://search.proquest.com/docview/1492736839?acco
untid=12085.

Woodard, Blair DeWitt. "Intimate Enemies: Visual Culture and
U.S.-Cuban Relations, 1945--2000." Order No.
3422400, The University of New Mexico, 2010. In
PROQUESTMS ProQuest Dissertations & Theses Full
Text,
http://search.proquest.com/docview/757372624?accou
ntid=12085.

Wu, H. D. Investigating the determinants of international news
flow: A meta-analysis. Gazette, 60 (6), 493-512.
(1998).

Wu, H. D. Systemic determinants of international news
coverage: A comparison of 38 countries. Journal of
Communication, 50 (2), 110-130. (2000).

Xing, Yi. "China's Panda Diplomacy: The Power of being
Cute." Order No. 1479963, University of Southern

California, 2010. In PROQUESTMS ProQuest Dissertations & Theses Full Text, http://search.proquest.com/docview/748221700?accou ntid=12085.

Yackley, Joseph. "Bankrupt: Financial Diplomacy in the Late Nineteenth-Century Middle East." Order No. 3557450, The University of Chicago, 2013. In PROQUESTMS ProQuest Dissertations & Theses Full Text, http://search.proquest.com/docview/1346014195?acco untid=12085.

Yan, Jing. "Is China's Outward FDI Politically Driven?" Order No. 1509015, Georgetown University, 2012. In PROQUESTMS ProQuest Dissertations & Theses Full Text, http://search.proquest.com/docview/1012104278?acco untid=12085.

Yoon, Y. Legitimacy, public relations, and media access: Proposing and testing a media access model. Communication Research, 32 (6), 762-793. (2005).

Yuan, Tian. "The New Great Leap Forward A Two-Case Analysis of Modern China's Efforts in External Communication Strategies." Order No. 1514188, University of Southern California, 2012. In PROQUESTMS ProQuest Dissertations & Theses Full Text, http://search.proquest.com/docview/1027917966?acco untid=12085.

Zajicek, Taylor Craig. "Modern Friendship: The "New Turkey" and Soviet Cultural Diplomacy, 1933-1934." Order No. 1563149, University of Washington, 2014. In PROQUESTMS ProQuest Dissertations & Theses Full Text, http://search.proquest.com/docview/1566673476?acco untid=12085.

Zatepilina, Olga. "Why U.S.-Based Nonprofit Organizations have a Stake in the U.S. Standing: A Case Study in Public Diplomacy." Order No. 3437589, Syracuse University, 2010. In PROQUESTMS ProQuest Dissertations & Theses Full Text, http://search.proquest.com/docview/821864565?accountid=12085.

About The Author

PhD. Jalal Nali was born in Tangier (Kingdom of Morocco) in 1975. He is an independent researcher in international affairs, public diplomacy strategies and experienced PR professional.

His perfect fluency in English, French, Spanish and Arabic makes his ground analysis precise and accurate. Before working as PR consultant strategist, Jalal gathered much valuable experience as consultant and advisor at private entities, he took office as projects manager, IT security consultant at most globally known IT firms, mostly in Europe; Mr. Nali is former president of Center of Peace and Development in the Mediterranean, former president of DPM, member of many international institutions as: Ana Lindh, Oxford research group on Terrorism, Geneva convention on armed violence and protection of civilians, MEED, author of many articles, reviewer at JEEM, and not last member of Crans Montana Forum (prized with 2014 award as leader of tomorrow).